Nathan Hubbell

My Journey to Jerusalem

Including Travels in England, Scotland, Ireland, France, Belgium...

Nathan Hubbell

My Journey to Jerusalem
Including Travels in England, Scotland, Ireland, France, Belgium...

ISBN/EAN: 9783744799010

Printed in Europe, USA, Canada, Australia, Japan

Cover: Foto ©Andreas Hilbeck / pixelio.de

More available books at **www.hansebooks.com**

JERUSALEM FROM THE MOUNT OF OLIVES.

MY JOURNEY TO JERUSALEM

INCLUDING

TRAVELS IN ENGLAND, SCOTLAND, IRELAND, FRANCE,
BELGIUM, GERMANY, HOLLAND, SWITZERLAND,
ITALY, GREECE, TURKEY, PALESTINE,
AND EGYPT

BY REV. NATHAN HUBBELL

"How hast thou purchased this experience? By my journey of observation."
—*Shakespeare.*

"Walk about Zion, and go round about her: tell the towers thereof Mark ye well her bulwarks, consider her palaces; that ye may tell it to the generation following."—*David.*

WITH 64 ILLUSTRATIONS

NEW YORK
PRINTED BY HUNT & EATON
150 FIFTH AVENUE
1890

Copyright 1890, by

NATHAN HUBBELL.

NEW YORK.

PREFACE.

"Do you believe in ghosts, Mr. Coleridge?" inquired a timid lady of that renowned and dreamy philosopher. "Madam," replied the poet, with great dignity, "I have seen too many ghosts in my day to believe in them."

The specious and morbid specters of doubt, want, and suspicion, in their multiform aspects, are still disturbers of the popular mind, not to name other dismal forebodings, whether believed in or not. Though well-nigh a life-long contributor to the department of periodical literature, besides much editorial labor, the author is not entirely devoid of interest concerning the possible financial fate that awaits this his first volume.

Geology graphically describes seven creative ages which characterized the formative processes of the earth, including notably the Azoic, Silurian, and Devonian. History alludes also to the ages of stone and iron, besides the dark and golden ages in the progress of civilization. Now, unfortunately, the age of fiction environs us. Vendors of the vitiating virus follow the unhappy tourist in his journeyings with the persistence of a sleuth-hound; it dominates the center-table and Sunday-school library, not unfrequently to the utter exclusion of standard works. Mr. Longfellow truthfully and epigrammatically asserts that "Many readers judge of the power of a book by the shock it gives their feelings, as some savage tribes determine the power of their muskets by their recoil, that being considered the best which prostrates the purchaser."

However, the Chautauquan and other modern educational movements have done much to turn the popular mind into soberer channels of thought. It is hoped that *My Journey to Jerusalem* may serve, in some degree at least, to facilitate the good work.

The book should not be confounded with exhaustive works on Palestine, since the writings of the Rev. Drs. W. M. Thomson, J. W. Mendenhall, H. B. Ridgaway, Bishop Newman, the Rev. Dr. F. S. De Hass, and others leave little if any thing to be desired. This is not its design. It is simply what its title implies, an account of the *journey*, its sights and significations, with personal impressions and adventures.

The trip to Jerusalem was made with the Fall

Palestine party, in 1889, organized by the writer; though space has been reserved for a description of other portions of Europe not included in the later itinerary, visited by him during a preliminary tour three years before. My original intention of furnishing also an account of four distinct visits to Canada in the present volume has been finally abandoned, since the size and expense of the work would be largely increased.

A large portion of the book was written while traveling in distant lands, as the several countries were passing in panoramic view before me. Nearly all of it has appeared in the form of foreign letters in the New Haven (Conn.) *Daily Journal and Courier.* For some reason all the correspondence from Palestine was suppressed by the Turkish government through the censor of the press. All private communications mailed at the same time and place were considerately allowed to reach their destination. Doubtless the suppressed manuscript contained some damaging disclosures which it was deemed important to conceal from the American people. While this narrow and tyrannical act of a tottering and bankrupt government imposed the unwelcome task of reproducing the confiscated letters, it furnished a favorable opportunity to verify dates and proper names, always a matter of extreme difficulty to the traveler in writing from foreign lands.

Mr. Carlyle, in *Sartor Resartus*, declares "The drop which thou shakest from thy wet hand rests not where it falls, but to-morrow thou findest it swept away; already on the wings of the north wind it is nearing the Tropic of Cancer." May the same potent and providential Hand that moves the forces of nature by such subtle agencies guide also the course of this plain and truthful narrative. In Sunday-school libraries and family circles every-where may it give the widest diffusion to a sound literature, and tend to win some wayward wanderer back to the fold of Jesus the Christ—the son of Mary and the Son of God!   NATHAN HUBBELL.

CONTENTS.

PAGE.

CHAPTER I.
FAREWELL GREETINGS.—PARSONS AND PUGILISTS ARE FELLOW-PASSENGERS!—LIFE ON THE ATLANTIC OCEAN..... 9

CHAPTER II.
STROLLS THROUGH LONDON, RUGBY, KENILWORTH CASTLE, AND THE PARIS EXPOSITION, WITH NOTES BY THE WAYSIDE.. 27

CHAPTER III.
RAMBLES IN WESTMINSTER ABBEY.—BUCKINGHAM PALACE.—A VISIT TO WINDSOR CASTLE.—"BANK HOLIDAY" AT OXFORD.—THE BANK OF ENGLAND.—STROLLS ABOUT LONDON—ENGLISH MANNERS AND CUSTOMS.—STRATFORD-ON-AVON.................................. 45

CHAPTER IV.
WANDERINGS IN EDINBURGH.—HOME AND CHURCH OF JOHN KNOX.—MELROSE ABBEY.—ABBOTSFORD AND SIR WALTER SCOTT.—GLASGOW.—SHIP-BUILDING ON THE CLYDE.—LAND O' BURNS AND TAM O' SHANTER............. 62

CHAPTER V.
THE BELFAST RIOTS.—IRELAND'S LARGEST LAKE.—CONCERNING CROWS.—BATTLE OF THE BOYNE.—JAUNTING-CAR RIDES.—DUBLIN AND ITS SIGHTS.—SIEGE OF DERRY, 1689.—GIANTS' CAUSEWAY........................ 82

CHAPTER VI.
OFF FOR PARIS.—A DISMAL NIGHT JOURNEY.—THE GAY METROPOLIS.—FALL OF THE BASTILE.—THE EXPOSITION OF 1889.—A CONTINENTAL SUNDAY.................. 106

CHAPTER VII.
BRUSSELS, THE GAY CAPITAL OF BELGIUM.—A VISIT TO THE BATTLE-FIELD OF WATERLOO.—GERMANY AND THE ROMANTIC RHINE.—HOLLAND, ITS PEOPLE, DIKES, AND WIND-MILLS.. 122

CONTENTS.

CHAPTER VIII.

ON TO SWITZERLAND.—MUSING ON THE MIGHTY ALPS.—LOVELY LUCERNE.—FLORENCE.—MILAN WITH HER MAJESTIC AND COSTLY CATHEDRAL.—THE ETERNAL CITY.—ROMAN RUINS AND MODERN ASPECTS.—A VISIT TO THE VATICAN.. 140

CHAPTER IX.

AT THE PALACE OF KING HUMBERT.—VESUVIUS VISITED.—EUROPEAN WARLIKE MOVEMENTS.—POMPEII RESURRECTED!—IMPRESSIONS OF GREECE................... 160

CHAPTER X.

DEPARTURE FOR SMYRNA.—THE LAND OF PASSPORTS.—A FEVER-SMITTEN CITY.—MOUNT PAGOS.—THE GRECIAN ARCHIPELAGO.—AN EXCURSION TO EPHESUS.—AT THE BIRTHPLACE OF SAUL............................... 179

CHAPTER XI.

BEYRUT.—CAMPING TOUR BEGINS.—AMERICAN COLLEGE.—FIRST NIGHT IN PALESTINE.—CHANGE OF PLAN.—MY LONELY JAUNT TO JERUSALEM....................... 207

CHAPTER XII.

FIRST IMPRESSIONS.—THE AMERICAN FAMILY.—SIGHTSEEING WITHIN AND AROUND THE WALLS.—GETHSEMANE.—THE MOUNT OF OLIVES.—BETHANY.—BETHLEHEM.—THE MOSQUE OF OMAR.—MODERN BUILDINGS, ETC.. 229

CHAPTER XIII.

KING SOLOMON'S FAMOUS MARBLE QUARRY.—ON TO EGYPT.—THE SUEZ CANAL.—EGYPTIAN MOSQUES AND WOMEN.—A VISIT TO THE SPHINX AND PYRAMIDS.—THE HOWLING DERVISHES......................... 262

CHAPTER XIV.

DEPARTURE FROM EGYPT.—"BLUES" ON THE BLUE MEDITERRANEAN.—VIEWS OF STROMBOLI.—SARDINIA, CORSICA, MARSEILLES, LYONS, ETC.—THE CRETAN INSURRECTION.—ARRIVAL IN NEW YORK.—FAREWELL OBSERVATIONS.. 292

ILLUSTRATIONS.

	Page
Jerusalem from the Mount of Olives	*Frontispiece.*
Rev. Nathan Hubbell	12
On Deck	18
Steamer's Dining-saloon	20
Nearing the Irish Coast	23
Kenilworth Castle	30
The Carpet-bagger in London	32
City Road Chapel	36
Interior of City Road Chapel	38
Charles Wesley's Tomb	40
Whitehall in the Days of James II	42
Susannah Wesley's New Tomb	43
Old Newgate Prison	47
Old London Bridge	49
Traitor's Gate, London Tower	51
Statue of Howard at St. Paul's	53
Quadrangle of Lincoln College, Oxford	55
Chapel of Lincoln College	55
St. Mary's Church, Oxford	57
The Broad Walk, Oxford	58
City of Edinburgh	64
John Knox	66
House of John Knox, Edinburgh	68
Thatched Cottage, Ireland	85
An Irish Hovel	88
Clarke's Monument, Portrush, Ireland	100
Louvre in the Sixteenth Century	110
Waterloo	128
Rhine Scenery	139
The Matterhorn	144

ILLUSTRATIONS.

	Page
Rome	151
Church at the Catacombs	154
Methodist Episcopal Church, Rome	158
Statue of Jupiter Olympus	174
Mars' Hill	176
Colossus of Rhodes	184
Theater at Ephesus Restored	193
Isle of Patmos	196
Tarsus	200
The Camping Tour	208
View of Beyrut	211
Bishop Kingsley's Monument	213
Sea of Galilee	216
A Caravan	220
Tower of Ramleh	226
The Mosque of Omar	232
Via Dolorosa	238
Interior of King Solomon's Temple	243
Mohammedans Worshiping	246
The Holy Sepulcher	249
A Bedouin	252
View from the Wall of Jerusalem	255
A Jerusalem Jew	259
On to Egypt	264
The Ark	269
On the Suez Canal	272
The Winged Lion	276
The Pyramids	278
The Sphinx	281
Entrance to the Great Pyramid	285
Hieroglyphics	289
Our Ship in a Gale	295
Moonlight on the Mediterranean	298
A Coral Island	302
Lyons	305
View of the Ocean	308

MY JOURNEY TO JERUSALEM.

CHAPTER I.

Ho! For Palestine.

FAREWELL GREETINGS.—PARSONS AND PUGILISTS ARE FELLOW-PASSENGERS!—LIFE ON THE ATLANTIC OCEAN.

> "Rock'd in the cradle of the deep,
> I lay me down in peace to sleep;
> Secure I rest upon the wave,
> For thou, O Lord, hast power to save.
> I know thou wilt not slight my call,
> For thou dost mark the sparrow's fall;
> And calm and peaceful is my sleep,
> Rock'd in the cradle of the deep."—*Emma Willard.*

> "I know not where His islands lift
>   Their fronded palms in air;
> I only know I cannot drift
>   Beyond his love and care."—*Whittier.*

AWAY from the mammoth and mighty city of New York, its superheated streets, "seven times hotter" than comfort or physical endurance demand, we sailed in the month of August. Two powerful steam-tugs by herculean efforts and incessant puffing finally succeed in towing the leviathan steamer *City of Rome* from her moorings to the channel.

On the pier the usual crowd, vast and demonstrative, is visible. Farewell words are whispered and handkerchiefs flutter like white-winged doves in the faint midsummer breeze. Amid the confusion of departure and the rush from the steamer when the hoarse shout of "All ashore that are going" is given, some exciting incidents occur. A portion of the luggage of a passenger falls into the dirty and rushing river. While it is being fished out with a boat-hook a great cry goes up—"A man overboard." It proves to be an unfortunate stevedore. A hundred willing hands are extended to save him. Doubtless they are successful, though we cannot tarry to learn the fact. The mighty ship is in motion. The powerful pulsations of her screw are felt, which will be our lullaby and morning salutation during the entire voyage of seven days or more. Down the harbor and bay we swiftly glide. The deafening din of the great metropolis—its pampered patricians of Wall Street, Murray Hill, and Fifth Avenue, who live in luxury, and the paupered plebeians of the "East side," who starve, steal, or die in dismal garrets and cellars, are left behind. Fainter and far away come voices from the receding city. Castle Garden, Bowling Green, Governor's Island, the lofty "Bartholdi Statue of Liberty Enlightening the World" are past. The beautiful shores of Staten

Island and Fort Hamilton are seen, with frowning forts on either side. Now we reach Quarantine and Sandy Hook. Here our pilot is discharged, and, in the judgment of very many, a great ocean race is begun, since the latest maritime wonders—the *City of New York* and *Teutonic*—sail at about the same hour as our steamer.

And now a new daily life is inaugurated. Instead of being "a night and a day on the deep," like Paul, a week or more must pass before land is sighted.

> "The hollow oak our palace is,
> Our heritage the sea."

Waiters are now styled "stewards," while baggage is transformed into "luggage," and "tips" are exchanged for courtesies. Sailing vessels, steam-tugs, fishing-boats, and finally pilot-boats, with huge numbers on their white sails, vanish, "Number Nineteen" being the last one visible. Before us, like Milton's serpent, "extended huge and vast and long," stretch three thousand miles of water. The sea is noticeably quiet. Save a gentle undulation it is as calm as the proverbial mill-pond. Later, during a storm, old Neptune exacted the customary tribute from many fellow-passengers, though I was personally exempt.

Only twenty of our Oriental party are on board, others having sailed before us, proposing to join the company at various points in Europe, including London, Paris, and Italy. Among the latter are the Rev. G. M. Stone, D.D., pastor of the Asylum Avenue Baptist Church, Hartford, Conn., and Newman Curtis, Esq., of Kentucky.

Much to the regret of myself and themselves,

REV. NATHAN HUBBELL.

Mr. A. H. Alling (the well-known manufacturer of hosiery and underwear, Birmingham, Conn.), and wife, were compelled to withdraw from the party a few days before the steamer sailed, owing to the death of Mrs. C. B. Alling, of that place, his brother's wife.

The passenger list revealed the fact that the party booked by the *City of Rome* was strictly cosmopolitan; Americans from California, Georgia, Montana, Illinois, Iowa—in fact, from nearly every State in the Union. There were English, Irish, Scotch, German, French, Norwegian, and African travelers, besides some from the West Indies and Australia.

From the latter point came Mr. Peter Jackson, the famous colored pugilist, with his manager, "Parson Davies." Mr. Jackson thus far has never been defeated. He is broad-shouldered, lithe, nimble as a kitten, and fully six feet two inches in height. He was on his way to fight "Jem Smith," the self-styled "Champion of England," whom he subsequently defeated with evident ease.

A large number of clergymen were on board, which possibly served to restore the social equilibrium. The utmost good order and courtesy prevailed throughout the entire voyage.

Four clergymen besides myself occupied one stateroom; the Rev. M. H. Plumb, of Illinois, a native of New Haven; the Rev. L. B. Edwards, Atlantic Highlands, N. J.; the Rev. W. Porteus, D.D., and the Rev. J. R. Armstrong (the latter two Presbyterians), of Missouri.

Meals were served sharply at half past seven A. M., twelve M. and five P. M., which were of a satisfactory character. How passengers dispose of their time for a week on the ocean is a problem to the uninitiated. Conversation, promenading on the upper deck, games of quoits and cards by some, reading from a well-furnished library, with occasionally a spice of flirtation, constitute some of the diversions usually employed. Three meals are served daily, with a lunch, in the second cabin, and four meals in the saloon.

The gigantic steamer carried comparatively few passengers—307 in all, of whom 105 were booked saloon, 152 second cabin, and 50 steerage. Even though the freight bills be added, it would seem quite impossible to meet the expenses of so large a vessel when we consider that 300 tons of coal are consumed daily, making a total for the trip of 2,400 tons. Add to this the wages of the officers and men, three hundred in number, who must also be fed three meals daily, and it will be apparent that but few men or corporations can indulge in the luxury of running an ocean steamer. The ship was built in 1881, is 565 feet in length, 8,415 tons register, with 12,500 horse-power, and 63 furnaces.

An excellent sermon was delivered in the main saloon on Sunday by the Rev. G. W. Huddleston (Methodist), of Cleveland, O., who goes with us through

Palestine and Egypt. His discourse evinced wide reading, a scholarly range of thought, and abounded in choice historical illustrations. A collection, according to usage, was then taken for the Home of Aged Mariners at Liverpool.

A religious service for seamen was also held in the afternoon in the open air on the main-deck, and another in the second cabin dining-saloon in the evening. A half hour prayer-meeting was likewise conducted daily on the spar-deck. Consequently, as will be seen, our religious privileges were exceedingly ample.

The speed of the vessel and the number of knots made per diem, our latitude and longitude, are subjects of deep interest to the average passenger. Not unfrequently bets are made regarding the number of miles made, which are officially decided at noon, when the daily log is posted at the saloon companion-way. Our average progress was about three hundred and eighty miles. While this seems slow in comparison with the later and improved steamers, *Etruria*, *City of New York*, and *Teutonic*, yet it exceeds the progress of a score of passenger steamers regularly crossing the Atlantic. What marvelous changes since Columbus crossed the ocean with his miniature and crazy crafts, consuming some three months of time! It should be borne in mind, however, that at least one more day must be added to the crack trips of five days and varying hours, of which we boast so much, before we gain our liberty and emerge from the custom-house, since the time is reckoned from Sandy Hook to Queenstown, two hundred and twenty miles being uncovered by the usual figures furnished. In sailing over the deep blue sea day after day, in pursuit of health, education, or pleasure, one is saddened to think of the bottom of the mighty ocean. Thousands of human beings are buried there. What a vast charnel-house! How many ships slumber beneath the restless wave!—the *President, Arctic, Oregon,* and a long list besides. How many homes have been blasted! How many hearts have been broken! What limitless treasures of silver, gold, and property of every description have gone down forever! And yet, annually, thousands sail over these waters thoughtlessly, carelessly, while the laugh, the jest, the wine-cup, and the merry dance go on. So men accumulate colossal fortunes or attain the summit of political power over the shattered hopes and blighted prospects of their fellow-men.

One of our Palestine party is the Rev. S. C. Upshaw, a colored clergyman of Atlanta, Ga. He is a graduate of Clark University, Presiding Elder of the Griffin District in that State, and editor of a local religious paper. For some cause he reached the dock after the steamer had left her pier at New York. Some would have abandoned the voyage in despair. But he is not that sort of man. Hiring a boatman for two dollars to convey him to the vanishing ship, he caught it in time; but, tendering a five-dollar bill to the man in the boat for change, the rascal rowed swiftly away with the entire amount, giving him curses instead of the money due him. Then he found that his overcoat had been left in a car of the elevated road, to add to his misfortunes—an article quite essential for comfort on the northern Atlantic. But, like Paul, "none of these things move him." His face is still " set toward Jerusalem." He expects to complete the Oriental trip, and tell the colored members of his district "what an ex-slave saw in Palestine" on his return.

Foggy weather was experienced for several days, which rendered the hoarse and repeated blasts of the fog-whistle an absolute necessity. Out of the murky gloom one morning we came within a "biscuit's toss" of a small fishing schooner, showing the imperative need of such precautions. The startled skipper evidently rejoiced over his narrow escape, for our modern leviathan would have sent him speedily to the bottom. Other vessels were occasionally sighted, some so remote from us as to seem mere specks on the distant horizon. In mid-ocean a lone stormy petrel, one of Mother Carey's chickens, as the sailor loves to call them, was met, fully twelve hundred miles from land. They are dreaded by sailors, who regard them with possibly some degree of superstitious awe, since their presence usually forebodes tempestuous weather. They will hover around ocean steamers

ON DECK.

night and day for a thousand miles or more, but are seldom molested.

The few steerage passengers on board, glad to escape the mephitic odors in their dank and dismal quarters, are seated on the dirty deck or lying prostrate fast asleep, with small children and infants by their side. A little tin trunk, or a well-worn basket, contains, in some instances, all their luggage. Love of kindred has again drawn them back to beautiful and oppressed Ireland, where home rule and misrule are engaged in the death-grapple for supremacy. May the day of deliverance speedily dawn!

The *City of Rome* is remarkably steady in a storm, which fact serves to attract passengers peculiarly susceptible to sea-sickness. Complaint has hitherto been made by some writers regarding the filthy condition of some portions of the vessel. Efforts toward cleanliness are largely confined to the saloon. Obviously much improvement could be made in the steerage if not in the intermediate department. The odors of a dozen water-closets penetrate the latter section of the steamer especially, while indications of general neglect are very manifest. If the popular commander, Captain Hugh Young, could occasionally visit each portion of the steamer during a voyage he would doubtless discover some remedy for these glaring abuses.

The vocabulary of the sailor includes slang and technical expressions, which are alike suggestive and amusing. Corned beef is described as "salt junk," "salt horse," and "old horse," according to the mood of Jack. Puddings composed of dried peas and boiled in a cloth are styled "dog's bodies," while hasty pudding is known as "loblolly." "Ship biscuit" is called, as in the army, "hard tack," and fresh wheat bread "soft tommy."

"Six water grog" implies much-diluted alcoholic drinks, and "to splice the main-brace" is to drink a larger quantity of the fiery fluid. "Half seas over" and "three sheets in the wind" denote the equivocal walk of the inebriate. "Bulling the barrel" is to add a quantity of water to the cask of liquor when it is low. "Sucking the monkey" is to suck liquor

STEAMER'S DINING-SALOON.

secretly through a gimlet-hole made in a full barrel of rum. A "lubber" is a green hand who has just begun a seafaring life. "Lubber's hole" is applied interchangeably to the hole in the maintop and to a sailor neglecting his duty. "Telling things to marines" suggests discredit when an improbable story is told. "Son of a sea cook" is applied in contempt to persons disliked, as is also the epithet "swab."

The man dealing out the grog is called a "bung-starter." The cook of a ship is known as "slushy," from his boiling salt pork called "slush." "A dirty dog and no sailor" is hurled at a lazy and villainous man. We have by no means exhausted the nautical vocabulary, but these illustrations must suffice.

Among the entertainments of the trip were concerts, lectures, and other exercises of an interesting character. Professor D. R. Dungan, of Drake University, Des Moines, Ia., presented a well-thought-out paper on "The Principles of Biblical Interpretation," and the Rev. A. P. Kriel, of Beaconsfield, South Africa, gave a vivid description of the diamond fields in that portion of the Dark Continent. The shafts sunk are from twelve to one thousand feet in depth, the shallower ones being near the bed of the river, where the gems have been washed down from distant elevations and buried in the sand. Natives employed in diamond digging work for two dollars and fifty cents per week, boarding themselves. Extraordinary vigilance is exercised to prevent the precious gems from being stolen. Every day, when labor is ended, the workmen are compelled to remove all their clothing and are critically examined to see that none are concealed therein, in their hair, mouths, under their arms, or between their toes. Formerly diamonds were secreted in old tin cans and thrown over the fence to a confederate, sold, and the proceeds divided. A tall fence just built renders the operation well-nigh impossible. Years ago diamonds were the property of any one finding them. Even children would hawk them about the streets, selling them for an insignificant sum. Now all the diamond-producing lands are owned by large companies, who guard their treasures in the strictest manner. Immense fortunes have been accumulated by the individual members of these corporations from the sale of diamonds, which find their way to Paris, London, New York, and other commercial centers of the world.

Long before port is reached the Yankee tourist is astonished at the erratic action of the sun, which persists in rising at eleven and twelve o'clock at night by New York time, when honest workers are presumably asleep—toilers on morning papers excepted. With his watch moved five hours ahead, he is at length prepared to begin wanderings in foreign lands.

The welcome cry of "Land Ho!" is heard! Fastnet light-house, at the entrance of St. George's Channel, is in view, while the rugged and barren mountains of Kerry are visible, though in dim outline. At Queenstown, Ireland, many passengers will leave

NEARING THE IRISH COAST.

us, and the Irish mail will be taken ashore. Thence, this chapter, written on a rocking ship amid the blasts of a furious gale and the swell of an angry sea, will, it is hoped, find its way to the intelligent readers of this volume of travels in due process of time. Our Oriental party will proceed to Liverpool, two hundred and twenty miles distant up St. George's Channel. Here we propose taking an early train for Kenilworth Castle, and pause a few hours to visit that venerable ruin. Then we push on to London, where the Sabbath, God willing, will be spent.

Now we are under the protection of Victoria, that estimable queen. Her extended reign has been of a pure and exalted character. The Prince of Wales, who, should he survive his mother, will succeed her in wearing the British crown, is now a man of mature years. The "wild oats" of his early career have been largely overcome, and by the masses forgotten. No one doubts his moral or intellectual fitness for this position of prominence and responsibility when the eventful period arrives.

The genealogy of Queen Victoria is traced as follows by a modern writer:

"Victoria, Queen of Great Britain and Empress of India, is the niece of William IV., who was the brother of George IV., who was the son of George III., who was the grandson of George II., who was the son of George I., who was the cousin of Queen Anne, who was the sister-in-law of William III., who was the son-in-law of James II., who was the brother of Charles II., who was the son of Charles I., who was the son of James I., who was the cousin of Elizabeth, who was the sister of Mary, who was the sister of Edward VI., who was the son of Henry VIII., who was the son of Henry VII., who was the cousin of Richard III., who was the uncle of Edward V., who was the son of Edward IV., who was the cousin of Henry VI., who was the son of Henry V., who was the cousin of Richard II., who was the grandson of Edward III., who was the son of Edward II., who was the son of Edward I., who was the son of Henry III., who was the son of John, who was the brother of Richard I., who was the son of Henry II., who was the cousin of Stephen, who was the cousin of Henry I., who was the brother of William Rufus, who was the son of William the Conqueror. Thus Queen Victoria can trace her ancestors back to about eight hundred years ago. It is the oldest reigning dynasty in the world."

She is the daughter of Edward, Duke of Kent, and was born at Kensington Palace, May 24, 1819.

A writer, speaking of the greatness of London, says: "Every four minutes marks a birth. In the next two hours after you read this thirty babies have been born and twenty deaths have taken place. Think of it! The evening paper that records the births and deaths of the preceding four-and-twenty hours must give three hundred separate items. Verily, its joys and sorrows are a multitude. London has seven thousand miles of streets, and if you walked them at the rate of twenty miles a day, you would have to walk almost a year, and more than a year by nearly fifty days, if you should rest on Sundays. And if you were a thirsty sort of a traveler, and couldn't pass a public-house, don't be alarmed—the seven thousand miles of streets have five-and-seventy miles of public-houses, so you need not think of thirst. In a year London folks swallow down 500,000 oxen, 2,000,000 sheep, 200,000 calves, 300,000 swine, 8,000,000 head of fowls, 500,000,000 pounds of fish, 500,000,000 oysters, 200,000,000 lobsters—is that enough to figure on? If not, there are some million tons of canned provisions, no end of fruit and vegetables, and 50,000,000 bushels of wheat. But how they wash all the food down you might feel glad to know. It takes 200,000,000 quarts of beer. But more than this, they drink 10,000,000 quarts of rum and 50,000,000 quarts of wine—the wine, the rum, the beer, 260,000,000 quarts."

CHAPTER II.

Strolls through London, Rugby, Kenilworth Castle, and the Paris Exposition, with Notes by the Wayside.

> "Britannia needs no bulwarks,
> No towers along the steep;
> Her march is o'er the mountain-waves,
> Her home is on the deep."—*Thomas Campbell.*

ON the damp, misty morning after our arrival at Liverpool, we drove rapidly through various portions of that vast commercial metropolis. The dull stone buildings, begrimed by the tarry touch of time and the incessant volumes of bituminous smoke from thousands of dwellings, factories, and public buildings, were gloomy in the extreme. Though the hour was early, long before breakfast, laboring men and women were hastening to their daily toil. Very many begin work at six A. M., before eating, and breakfast between eight and nine o'clock. Conversing with some of them, they proved to be intelligent, cheerful, and apparently contented with their earthly condition. All showed the deepest interest in America, particularly in the salaries received by our mechanics and other wage-earners.

A glance at the amounts paid in England should

forever remove the cobwebs of the free-trade delusion from the minds of thoughtful men. Let a few illustrations suffice, which are furnished by a competent authority:

Conductors on trams (street-cars) and omnibuses are paid $6 72 per week and work sixteen hours a day, having no Sunday rest. Policemen in London receive $5 76 a week, firemen the same amount, while laboring-men must be content with $4 32. Printers toil fifty-four hours a week in Sunderland for $7 20; blacksmiths, fifty-three hours for $7 56; carpenters, for the same time, $7 68; brick-layers and stone-masons, fifty hours for $7 98; tailors, fifty-five hours for $5 50; and engineers, fifty-four hours for a stipend of $7 68.

The massive granite docks and piers at Liverpool have for years attracted the attention of American tourists especially. Solidity and durability are their prominent characteristics. The cost, though vast, embracing several millions of dollars, has been a wise investment. Above three hundred acres are covered by them, besides perhaps twenty miles of quays.

Few objects of interest detain us at Liverpool. Her public buildings are immense, and built as a rule of enduring granite. Various statues to men prominent in English history adorn the plazas and public parks. In 1886 we visited her great "Exposition," then in progress. Though restful to the traveler after a protracted sea voyage, and creditable to the nation, yet it presented comparatively few novelties contrasted with our gigantic display at Philadelphia in 1876. Hungry for greater attractions elsewhere in Europe, the average traveler pushes rapidly on.

Rugby was our next point of interest. Two hours were spent in delightful rambles through its quaint and quiet streets, its charming hedge-rows, cozy cottages, and wealth of foliage. Of course, the famous grammar school of the late Dr. Thomas Arnold was seen, and perhaps with a superabundance of Yankee rashness I sat in the private chair of that eminent man, and even ascended the pulpit in the chapel. Near Rugby Addison once lived. *Tom Brown's School Days, The Manliness of Christ,* and other works of genial and gifted Thomas Hughes come naturally to mind as we gaze about the venerable structure or stroll through the quiet streets.

The ashes of Arnold repose in the memorial tomb at Rugby Chapel. At the time of his death he had barely entered his forty-seventh year. Fifteen years after being deposited in their final resting-place, his son, Matthew, published a poem, written by himself, a filial tribute to the memory of his distinguished father, the opening stanza of which is as follows:

"O strong soul, by what shore
Tarriest thou now? For that force,
Surely, has not been left vain!
Somewhere, surely, afar,
In the sounding labor-house vast
Of being, is practiced that strength,
Zealous, beneficent, firm!"

KENILWORTH CASTLE.

Arnold's reputation as an instructor, a fearless polemic, a historian, and a profound and polished classical scholar will long survive him.

Kenilworth Castle then drew us reluctantly away. The history of this interesting ruin covers a period of possibly a thousand years. Facts regarding it are comparatively few, while traditions abound. Founded by Geoffrey de Clinton, Lord Chamberlain to Henry I., it in succession became the property of Henry III., Simon de Montfort, Earl of Leicester, John of Gaunt, Henry IV., and many more. Here Edward II. suffered imprisonment. It was also owned by Queen Elizabeth, who finally gave it to Dudley, the Earl of Leicester, a special favorite at the palace, who squandered $85,000 during an entertainment lasting seventeen days.

Over the green, grassy slopes about the castle many monarchs have strolled in their moments of leisure. What vast aggregations of beauty, wealth, valor, and regal power, which ever and anon in the shadowy past were attracted to the spot, do these ivy-clad walls suggest! Gone! Gone! "What shadows we are, and what shadows we pursue!"

From the summit of the crumbling ruin extended and delightful views are afforded. Well trimmed hedge-rows, broad fields of verdant loveliness, with stretches of charming English landscape, attract the eye. But we may not tarry. Thousands of miles, by land and sea, yet to be traversed call us away from the scene, and we hasten by a rapid train.

LONDON.—Negress night had drawn her somber curtain o'er earth and sky around the mighty metrop-

THE CARPET-BAGGER IN LONDON.

olis, when our party alighted. Carriages are in readiness, and away we speed for Covent Garden Hotel.

London, situated on the Thames, 60 miles from the sea, covers an area of streets and squares embracing 122 square miles. The population is about 4,500,000, including 120,000 foreigners; it contains more Roman Catholics than Rome, and more Jews than Palestine. The police force numbers over 10,700 men. In various directions there are more than ten continuous miles of houses. The water supply averages 50,000,000 gallons daily, and 400,000 gas lamps light its streets, consuming 15,000,000 cubic feet of gas every day. The coal consumed annually is estimated at 5,500,000 tons, and the annual rental at £20,000,000. On an average 28 miles of new streets and 9,000 new houses are erected yearly. Every day sees about 160,000 strangers enter the city, and 123 persons are daily added to its population by birth.

The great city seems substantially the same as we left it three years ago. The push of the bustling multitude, the roar of 'buses, trams, and other vehicles are unchanged. And yet London, like all great business centers, varies like the kaleidoscope. Death does its direful work. Reverses overtake the oldest mercantile houses, while emigration and immigration alike forbid any approach to stagnation. Hence, Tennyson's "Song of the Brook," modified, might read,

"Men may come and men may go,
But London goes on forever."

The formidable strike of the dock laborers was in progress. All phases of the subject received ample treatment, not only in the local press, including the *Times*, *Telegraph*, and other publications, but by the public generally. From the tops of 'buses and trams, within coffee-houses and beer-shops, even along the corridors of the Bank of England and the Royal Exchange, it was the teeming topic. Whitechapel, amid its horde of horrors, and West End, in rustling silk and costly broadcloth, talked it over. Even at Westminster Abbey on Sunday, and in other pulpits, the officiating clergymen alluded to it in conciliatory terms, and counseled moderation and peace on the part of the people, especially the working-men.

Our party roamed *ad libitum* throughout the metropolis without attempting unity of action. The National Gallery of Art, British Museum, Tower of London, with the thousand and one objects of interest abounding on every hand, were drawn upon freely.

Personally, the gallery was a disappointment. Few modern pictures were there, while scores on exhibition were valued more for the historical associations connected with them than for intrinsic merit. A superabundance of paintings which had done service for long years at cathedrals and elsewhere were exhibited, presenting the infant Jesus, the Madonna and Child, the Magi, repeatedly. To my unartistic vision nothing could be more out of taste than the utterly improbable posture of painting the infant Jesus in a state of nudity on the floor, while Mary, Joseph, and the Wise Men gaze upon him with evident admiration. The paintings of Landseer and Rosa Bonheur, on the contrary, were an exquisite delight.

The Colonial and Indian Exhibition, London, in progress during our first visit, proved a gratifying success. Immense audiences thronged the place daily. At night the number was estimated at from thirty to fifty thousand within the park and buildings. Thousands of minute colored lights burned and twinkled in the darkness overhead, on the borders of the paths, amid the foliage of the trees by the waters of the fountains. Large and numerous electric lights also blazed brilliantly at various points on the grounds, presenting a scene of rare beauty.

The single Sabbath at our disposal included services at City Road Chapel (Wesleyan) in the morning, Westminster Abbey in the afternoon, and Spurgeon's Tabernacle at night. The former church is the Methodist Mecca, founded and built by John Wesley, his old pulpit being still there. His house, writing-desk and famous tea-pot next door, with his grave in the rear of the church, explain, in some degree at least, the denominational interest in the locality.

Wesley's tea-pot is highly valued as a relic. It is composed of chinaware, so-called, blue and white, and is of

CITY ROAD CHAPEL.

huge proportions. A part of the spout has been knocked off. It bears the following inscriptions, the first being now generally sung at Wesleyan public tea-meetings before meals, and the second one at the close:

> "Be present at our table, Lord,
> Be here and every-where adored;
> These creatures bless, and grant that we
> May feast in Paradise with thee."

On the reverse side is the following:

> "We thank thee, Lord, for this, our food,
> But more because of Jesus' blood;
> Let manna to our souls be given,
> The bread of life sent down from heaven."

Cyrus W. Field has made a standing offer of $2,500 for the tea-pot, and Mr. Peck, of the firm of Peck & Snyder, New York, has recently offered $5,000 for the relic without avail. Evidently some crockery is held at a high valuation.

By the side of Wesley sleep Rev. Jabez Bunting and Rev. Richard Watson, conspicuous theologians of their day. There is also a monument to the memory of Rev Dr. Adam Clarke, whose Commentary on the Scriptures, the product of forty years of tireless toil, is still unrivaled in the judgment of many mature lay and clerical minds.

Across the street from City Road Chapel lies the body of John Bunyan, the immortal dreamer, in Bunhill Fields Cemetery. The original tombstone has long since disappeared. Vandals from many lands have removed it in a fragmentary form as souvenirs. Now an iron monument of graceful propor-

INTERIOR OF CITY ROAD CHAPEL.

tions marks the spot. Panels, with views chosen from suggestions contained in *Pilgrim's Progress*, appropriately adorn each side of the shaft.

Isaac Watts, the Christian poet; Daniel Defoe, author of *Robinson Crusoe, Memoirs of a Cavalier, New Voyage Around the World, Political History of the Devil*, and other publications; Susannah Wesley, mother of nineteen children, two of whom, John and Charles Wesley, achieved world-wide distinction; and many conspicuous characters besides, rest within the inclosure. It is probably the oldest grave-yard in the city. Some of the tombstones have strange and weird faces carved upon them, with inscriptions no less peculiar. One stone bears the following announcement: "Here lies the body of Dame Mary Page. From her were taken two hundred and forty gallons of water in sixty-seven months, during which she was tapped sixty-six times."

Newman Hall still draws immense audiences at his church on Westminster Road. It is a favorite resort of American visitors. He is a great friend of the United States. The steeple of the church is known as Lincoln Tower, and was built largely by funds contributed by his friends in America, during a visit to his intimate friend, the Rev. Dr. Theodore L. Cuyler, of Brooklyn. It is in honor of Abraham Lincoln and the Emancipation Proclamation, and con-

CHARLES WESLEY'S TOMB.

tains red, white, and blue stones. The anniversary of Mr. Hall's church was being celebrated, and the sermon proved one of great excellence.

Mr. Spurgeon did not appear at his best. His step was slow and heavy, he being still the victim of rheumatic gout. During both the morning and evening services the devotional exercises and Scripture reading were conducted by assisting clergymen, the Rev. Joseph Spurgeon, his brother, officiating at night. Like his gifted relative, he possesses a voice of marvelous clearness and compass, but beyond this there is no legitimate comparison.

Owing to the fact that the Lord's Supper was to be celebrated at the close, Mr. Spurgeon preached but forty minutes. As a rule he exceeds one hour, however. While the discourse contained many interesting points, it was an intellectual effort far below his usual standard. He seemed to be aware of the fact, for both morning and evening he made apologetic allusions to the subject. His church is fully conscious of the precarious condition of his health, and as much of the routine work of the parish as is practicable is performed by fully qualified assistants.

Spurgeon's Bible readings, with spicy comments interspersed, as a rule surpass his sermons in interest. A few expressions, heard during my previous visit to Europe, three years before, still linger in the chambers of memory. Speaking on the "Highway of Holiness," he said, "The best 'way' God shows us is a safe way out of the world." "Don't you understand that?" said he, at another point; "why, it is as plain as a pike-staff, as plain as the nose on your face." The man with a huge proboscis before him evidently felt

WHITEHALL IN THE DAYS OF JAMES II.

that his personal nose had caught the great preacher's eye, much to his mortification.

The administration of the Lord's Supper was a memorable sight. On a large oblong table were thirty-eight plates of bread and about sixty cups of wine, the silver service presenting a beautiful appearance by gas-light. He follows the biblical narrative in the exercises, and in the distribution of the emblems in a large degree.

SUSANNAH WESLEY'S NEW TOMB.

The ceremony is properly observed in the evening. The bread is broken, not cut into cubes, as is quite common in America, at least. Prayer is offered, c thanks are given, and a hymn sung, as suggested by the New Testament account. He gave the emblems to twelve deacons, representing the twelve apostles, who give to the multitude. The Tabernacle will hold twelve thousand people, and fully twenty-five hundred, if not more, remained at the after-service to participate.

Secret but persevering efforts are still being made by the London police to ferret out "Jack the Ripper," the supposed perpetrator of the numerous Whitechapel murders. The entire detective force, stimulated by the various offers of reward and the reproaches of the public press and the people generally, is in motion. Private meetings are held by those in authority, at which every hint or possible suggestion is duly weighed. Even dreams are related, and, if considered of importance, receive careful investigation. Finally the British lion has been thoroughly aroused. Justice is on the track of the most blood-thirsty assassin of modern times. Sooner or later his arrest will follow. Unless he proves to be a murderous maniac, as many believe, he will speedily expiate his crimes on the gallows.

CHAPTER III.

RAMBLES IN WESTMINSTER ABBEY.—BUCKINGHAM PALACE.—A VISIT TO WINDSOR CASTLE.—"BANK HOLIDAY" AT OXFORD.—THE BANK OF ENGLAND.—STROLLS ABOUT LONDON.—ENGLISH MANNERS AND CUSTOMS.—STRATFORD-ON-AVON.

> "The pilgrim spirit has not fled;
>   It walks the noon's broad light;
> It watches the bed of the glorious dead,
>   With the holy stars by night.
> It watches the bed of the brave who have bled,
>   And shall guard the ice-bound shore
> Till the waves of the bay where the *Mayflower* lay
>   Shall foam and freeze no more!"

WESTMINSTER ABBEY, London, is a vast and venerable mausoleum of the most conspicuous monarchs, statesmen, poets, authors, divines, artists, and military chieftains of earth. It was begun during the reign of Henry III., and finally finished by the continuous action of Edward I. and Henry VII., respectively. Sir Christopher Wren, the celebrated English architect, designer of St. Paul's Cathedral which cost £747,954, planned the western towers. This great man was buried in the crypt of St. Paul's. A black marble slab contains this simple but suggestive inscription, "*Si monumentum requiris, circumspice*"—meaning, "If you seek his monument, look around."

The abbey is 530 feet long, width at the transept 203 feet; the height of the western towers is 225 feet. On Sundays services open to the public are conducted at three o'clock P. M. and other hours. The singing of the large choir of boys and masculine voices is simply wonderful. Unless one comes early and secures a seat well forward it is almost impossible to understand more than a few words of the sermon. Cathedrals are built for show rather than for their acoustic properties. On Mondays and Tuesdays admission is free to all parts of the building. Sixpence fee is required to visit the sepulcher of the kings and other parts of the building. On other days no fee is required. A great curiosity at the abbey, the coronation chair or "throne used in the coronation ceremonies of the kings and queens of Great Britain, and which is so splendid in its covering of rich silks, velvet, and gold, is, in fact, simply an old oaken chair of antique pattern. It has been used on all state occasions for the last six hundred years, and perhaps even longer, many reputable writers claiming that they have discovered traces of its existence prior to the eleventh century. Ages of use have made the old oaken frame-work as hard and as tough as iron. The back and sides of this throne-chair were formerly painted in various colors. These parts are now hidden by heavy hangings of satin, silk, and velvet. The magic powers attributed to the old relic lie in the

OLD NEWGATE PRISON.

seat, which is made of a heavy, rough-looking sandstone, 26 inches in length, $17\frac{1}{2}$ inches in width, and $19\frac{1}{2}$ inches in thickness. Long before it was wrapped in velvet and trimmed in gold, to be used by the

Tudors and the Stuarts, this old stone of stones served as a seat during the coronations of the early Scottish kings."

"The Bank of England was founded in 1694, and is the largest monetary establishment in the world. It employs nearly one thousand clerks. In the bullion office is an ingenious apparatus for weighing gold and silver, and in the weighing office is a machine for weighing sovereigns, by which thirty-five thousand separate coins can be weighed in a day by a single machine. There are ingenious steam machines for printing the bank-notes and marking them in microscopic writing. Over the drawing office is a clock having sixteen dials. The collection of ancient coins, the bank-note printing machinery, and the bullion cellars can be seen by an order, for which application in writing should be made to the secretary. Orders can also be procured through the manager of any London bank for a customer of such bank and his friends. The public are at liberty to walk through the offices from nine till four."

QUEEN'S PALACES.—Buckingham Palace, London, near St. James Park, is the residence of the queen when in the city. It is seldom opened to the public, but contains a superb collection of paintings by noted artists. Queen Victoria's summer-house in her private garden is decorated with choice frescoes by

Eastlake, Maclise, Landseer, Stanfield, and other well-known painters.

Windsor Castle is twenty-two miles west from London by the road through Brentford. It may be reached in an hour or less by the Great Western Railway from Paddington, or the South-western from Waterloo. Windsor occupies a rising ground on the

OLD LONDON BRIDGE.

south bank of the Thames, and is interesting for its ancient and extensive castle, the grandest royal residence in Great Britain. In the lower court is St. George's Chapel, an elegant Gothic edifice, in which service is performed on Sundays, occasionally in presence of the royal residents. Besides the chapel and keep, the chief parts of the castle attractive to strangers are the state apartments in the upper or northern court; these are exhibited free to visitors, during the absence of the court, on Mondays, Tuesdays, Thursdays, and Fridays, between the hours of eleven and three in winter, and eleven and four in summer. Tickets can be obtained at the principal shops in London or of the Lord Chamberlain on the royal premises.

I spent a delightful day in my trip to Windsor Castle, being obliged to defer it for some time. I finally gained admission, as it is never opened to visitors when occupied by the queen. Passing near Buckingham Palace on my return to London, which the guard in uniform stated was never exhibited to the public, I passed two young ladies on horseback. They were daughters of the Prince of Wales, the same authority told me. The horses—beautiful dapple grays—he described as the "royal stud." The animals were in fine condition, and the young ladies proved excellent riders. They were returning from a morning jaunt in St. James Park, which is near the palace. Each wore a dark riding-dress, and they were conversing in an animated manner and smiling. Their faces were somewhat thin and bore an expression of sadness.

At the Young Men's Christian Association, London, I made a brief call asking the privilege of examining certain American religious newspapers, especially *The Christian Advocate*, published at New York. My request was courteously granted, though I was promptly informed that the rooms were not open to the public as in America, but for members only, the

TRAITOR'S GATE, LONDON TOWER.

attendant remarking in conclusion that "our system would not answer at all for London."

Judge of my surprise, however, on learning, as I did, that the only religious paper taken from America was the Boston *Watchman*, a denominational publication. One would think that the various branches of religious thought would scarcely be content with so limited a range of vision, notwithstanding its excellent matter and management.

In Stratford, East London. I discovered a well-executed and costly monument erected to the memory of eighteen Protestant martyrs who were burned at the stake near its site in 1555. Eleven men and two women were consumed in one fire. One of the men was totally blind. Twenty thousand spectators, according to the inscription on the monument, witnessed the execution. Several suggestive and appropriate passages of Scripture were added to the historical account on the shaft, including, "They overcame by the blood of the Lamb, and the word of their testimony," and, "They loved not their lives unto death."

The "Fire Monument," built in memory of the furious and terrible fire of London, known as the "Great Fire," is two hundred and two feet high. It was designed by Sir Christopher Wren. From the summit a surpassing and extensive view of London is afforded. A nominal fee of threepence is required to secure admission.

Oxford was visited on my return from the Continent. The day chosen was unpropitious, it being "Bank holiday" in England, when nearly all public and private buildings are closed. A regatta was an-

STATUE OF HOWARD AT ST. PAUL'S.

nounced to take place on the Thames in the afternoon, which attracted a large crowd of ladies and gentlemen to its banks in holiday attire.

The city contains twenty or more institutions of learning, which constitute largely the life of the place. Shops, boarding-houses, and hotels depend on the patronage of the students chiefly for existence. Manufacturing, if at all, is conducted on a limited scale.

Among the curiosities shown at the Ashmolean Museum are Cromwell's watch and privy seal; also, Henry VIII.'s sword, bearing the inscription, "Defender of the Faith," which was presented him by the pope. Considering the subsequent quarrel between that much-married monarch and the pope, his widely known excommunication, and the ultimate formation of the Church of England as a result of that protracted dispute, the term seemed quite suggestive. Also, a pair of bellows once owned by Charles II., a gauntlet glove worn by Mary Queen of Scots, the riding-boots of Queen Elizabeth, the spurs of Charles I., King Alfred's jewel (regarded as a great curiosity), the steel band that bound Cranmer to the stake when he was burned alive in 1556, a piece of charred oak, a portion of the stake to which Latimer and Ridley were fastened when they suffered death by fire, and a cloak of deer-skins, gayly decorated with beads, worn by Powhatan, the father of Pocahontas.

QUADRANGLE OF LINCOLN COLLEGE, OXFORD.

CHAPEL OF LINCOLN COLLEGE.

Oxford has sent forth to the world an army of educated men, many of whom have achieved an enviable distinction, including John Wesley, a fellow of Lincoln College, and William E. Gladstone.

To American eyes it was a decided novelty to witness, as I did, many women of apparent respectability, accompanied by their escorts, and in some cases by children, at the public bars drinking beer and wine amid a crowd of men.

In other particulars manners and customs in England differ widely from ours. During the entire summer I have seen ladies and misses with straw bonnets, light-colored dresses, and yet wearing fur capes over their shoulders. At first I supposed that they were worn for ornament, but was assured later that they were used as a protection from the damp weather and sudden changes of the atmosphere. For the same cause black hats were worn generally by the gentlemen. Wearing a dark straw hat when I left New York, I found myself a conspicuous object in Great Britain and elsewhere. Street-cars—or trams, as they are called here—and the 'buses have seats for twenty passengers on top besides the usual number within. All vehicles keep to the left instead of the right as in America, the rule applying to steam railways also.

Drinking-water was difficult to obtain throughout

ST. MARY'S CHURCH, OXFORD.

Europe. In no railway station or hotel did I obtain water without asking for it; none accessible to all as with us. When brought it uniformly came in a

THE BROAD WALK, OXFORD.

decanter, and was nearly tepid. Ice apparently had dwindled to the vanishing point. A gentleman traveling with me paid one penny (two cents) for a glass of water without ice.

The prices of sugar in England seemed ridiculously low. Loaf-sugar cut in cubes retails at twopence — four cents—a pound, while a light brown sugar is sold for three cents a pound. Choice mixed candy in many places sells for eight cents a pound—fourpence. The English youth is thereby enabled to **supply his girl with confectionery** at a nominal price every Sabbath evening, possessing thereby a decided advantage over his American cousin.

Bootblacks in Liverpool and London wear a scarlet uniform, a number, and are licensed. Other boys in uniform, with a brush and a sort of wooden dustpan, plunge constantly among the passing vehicles, at the risk of limb and life, to remove the horse-droppings, so that the street may be in fair condition.

CHESTER.—A brief visit was made at Chester, seventeen miles from Liverpool. Both cities were included in our itinerary of 1886. Founded by the Romans before Christ, according to some ancient authorities, Chester presents many ancient structures, with a portion of the wall that once environed the city, including modern residences of a tasteful and attractive character. Horse railroads run through the center of the place, the tops of the cars furnishing a convenient and economical mode of seeing the chief points of interest.

Stratford-on-Avon was reached late at night. Some

difficulty was experienced in securing accommodations, the hotels being crowded. The Golden Lion Hotel at length made room for us. A political meeting relative to home rule and the Gladstone movement was just closing. Lord Dutton, I understood the name to be, was conveyed by his party adherents to our hotel in an open carriage. Of course, a great throng was attracted to the spot, which rendered it necessary to defer the matter of sleep. After singing "He's a Jolly Good Fellow," and several other rousing songs, the crowd slowly departed after repeatedly drinking the health and success of his lordship.

Shakespeare's house, the Memorial Hall, and the church where his body reposes were duly visited the following day, preceded by a delightful morning stroll on the banks of the quiet and beautiful Avon. The old, old verse came again and again to my mind as I sat in a little boat on the celebrated river:

> "The Avon to the Severn runs,
>   The Severn to the sea,
> And Wiclif's dust is spread abroad
>   Wide as the waters be."

A long arch of tree-tops of great beauty, resembling the classic, poetic, and dreamy appearance of Temple Street, which crosses "The Green," New Haven, Conn., shelters the visitor as he approaches the church. Entering the small oaken door cut into a larger one, you are compelled to bow to avoid a blow on the head. Why the door was constructed so low it is difficult to tell, unless it was to induce involuntary reverence. A thump on the cranium of a careless person would be likely to evoke emotions quite the reverse of devotion, however.

The tomb of Shakespeare remains undisturbed within the chancel, where his wife is also buried by his side. Possibly the curse hurled at the reckless relic-hunter in the rude rhyme on the slab has deterred the peripatetic vandal from chronic rashness. These familiar lines, with their antiquated spelling, still remain distinctly carved on the plain marble slab covering the ashes of the world's greatest dramatist and delineator of character, and are as follows:

> "Good frend for Iesus sake forbeare
> To digg the dust encloased heare :
> Blest be ye man yt spares these stones,
> And curst be he yt moves my bones."

Quaint and well-executed carvings appear on many of the seats of the ancient church, including vines, flowers, and grotesque heads of various descriptions. Some of the figures, strangely enough, are grossly indecent. It is difficult to understand the motive or taste that would cause them to be placed permanently in any building at any period in the history of the world—especially in a place of worship.

CHAPTER IV.

WANDERINGS IN EDINBURGH.—HOME AND CHURCH OF JOHN KNOX.—MELROSE ABBEY.—ABBOTSFORD AND SIR WALTER SCOTT.—GLASGOW.—SHIP-BUILDING ON THE CLYDE.—LAND O' BURNS AND TAM O' SHANTER.

> "November's sky is chill and drear,
> November's leaf is red and sear;
> Late, gazing down the steepy lin
> That hems our little garden in,
> Low in the dark and narrow glen,
> You scarce the rivulet might ken,
> So thick the tangled greenwood grew,
> So feeble trilled the streamlet through;
> Now murmuring hoarse and frequent seen,
> Through bush and briar, no longer green,
> An angry brook, it sweeps the glade,
> Brawls over rock and wild cascade,
> And, foaming down with doubled speed,
> Hurries its waters to the Tweed."—*Sir Walter Scott.*

AT Edinburgh, in 1886, the great exhibition was still in progress. Vast crowds, attracted by the mammoth fair, surged through the streets and thronged the wide corridors of the exhibition buildings. Every train increased the mass of humanity to uncomfortable proportions. The hotels were more than full, while landlords and waiters were, if possible, more independent and brusque than ever.

"Shakedowns" and improvised beds of every description were placed in the parlors, dining-rooms, and odd corners and nooks of the cheaper hotels especially to accommodate the influx of guests.

The display of goods at the exhibition was highly respectable, though few novelties were discovered. Having just seen the Colonial and Indian Exhibition at London and the great Liverpool Fair, besides our gigantic exposition at Philadelphia in 1876, as already stated elsewhere, the exhibits obviously could not produce startling effects on me. At Holyrood Palace ample preparations were making for the expected visit of the queen, which occurred a week later.

The process of lithographic printing was shown at the fair; also the composition and press-work required on established journals, some of which are regularly issued from the grounds. Scarfs for the ladies, manufactured on the spot, of flexible glass thread in variegated hues, were quite attractive, non-breakable, and as pliable as cloth. They were sold at prices ranging from sixty to eighty-six cents of our currency. We saw them also at the Liverpool buildings.

The old manse, or parsonage, of John Knox on High Street, Edinburgh, is still visited by tourists. The building has recently been put in thorough repair, though the antique aspect is preserved. Old-fashioned furniture of by-gone centuries is found in

CITY OF EDINBURGH.

each room; but one or two articles, however, are positively known to have been used by the sturdy reformer—his study-chair and possibly a writing-desk. From a side window opening on the busy street Knox frequently preached to an immense congregation of eager listeners that stood without. Adjoining the venerable structure stands the church bearing his name. It is a modern building, though the descendants of the families to whom he formerly preached still worship there. A Sabbath morning was profitably spent in listening to the present incumbent—a man of deep thought, excellent voice and presence. Strangely enough, though the day was exceptionally fine, the entire audience consisted of but fifty-three persons. Contributions for current expenses were deposited on a large silver plate, which was conspicuously displayed in the vestibule at the front door, guarded by two officers of the church. The same custom prevailed at "Dr. Guthrie's church," as it is still called, where I listened to a plain, practical discourse by his successor on the same afternoon. In Roman Catholic churches in some portions of Europe the collection-boxes are extended to the people as they assemble before the services by young men standing on the sidewalk.

The following inscriptions were found on the windows of the John Knox church near the pulpit:

"John Knox, born 1509; died 1572." "Thomas Chalmers, born 1780; died 1847."

The following letter from John Knox to Mrs. Bowes will prove of interest to many. It is taken

JOHN KNOX.

from the *Life of John Knox*, by the late Charles K. True, D.D., and published by Cranston & Stowe, Cincinnati. As a souvenir of those stormy and heroic days, it is printed entire with its quaint and original Scotch spelling:

"The wayis of man ar not in his awn power. Albeit my journey toward Scotland, belovit mother, was maist contrarious to my awn judgement before I did interpryse the same; yet this I praise God for thame wha was the cause externall of my resort to these quarteris; that is, I prais God in yow and for yow, whom hie maide the instrument to draw me from the den of my awn case (you allane did draw me from the rest of quyet studie), to contemplat and behald the fervent thirst of oure brethrene, night and day sobbing and gronyng for the breid of lyfe. If I had not sene it with my eis, in my awn contry, I cauld not have beleveit it.

"I praisit God, when I was with you, perceaving that in the middis of Sodome, God had mo Lottis than one, and ma faithful doctheris than tua. But the ferveneie heir dioth fer exceid all utheris that I have seen. And thairfoir ye sall pacientlie bear altho' I heir yet some dayis; for depart I can not unto sic tyme as God quenche thair thrist a litill. Yea, mother, their fervencie doith sa ravische me that I can not but a accus and condemp my sleuthful coldness. God grant thame thair —— hartis desyre; and I pray you adverteis me of your estait, and of thingis that have occurit sence your last wrytting. Comfort your self in Godis promissis, and be assureit that God steiris up mo frendis than we be war of. My com-

HOUSE OF JOHN KNOX, EDINBURGH.

mendation to all in your company. I commit you to the protectionn of Omnipotent. In great haist; the 4, of November, 1555. From Scotland.

"Your sone,

"JOHNE KNOX."

"The Castle" occupies a commanding site, several angles and sides being nearly as difficult of access as Gibraltar itself. A view of surpassing beauty greets one from the fortification. The silver waters of the Firth of Forth sparkled beneath the rays of the afternoon sun, which was fast sinking beyond the western hill-tops. Edinburgh, with the broad and beautiful Princess Street, George Street, parks and buildings, stretched like a panorama before me. A beautiful perspective of distant and highly cultivated fields, with a wealth of well-kept hedgerows and Scottish mountains in the background, lent an additional charm to the scene. A wild and rocky ravine, once an eyesore, running through Edinburgh has been transformed into a lovely park. The crown jewels of the early sovereigns of Scotland, and those now worn on state occasions, are deposited at the castle and guarded with the utmost vigilance. Sir William Kirkoldy bravely defended the castle for Mary, Queen of Scots, for a period of thirty-three days, with an inferior force, against the united armies of both England and Scotland. The immense cannon, twenty inches in diameter, which did excellent service at the siege of Norham Castle in 1514, is exhibited as one of the curiosities of the spot. For one hundred and fifty years it was on exhibition at the Tower of London, but by the command of George IV. it was returned to the castle in 1829. It was forged at Mons in 1496. The garrison in their neat and picturesque Highland costume presented an attractive appearance, especially to the eyes of the rustic visitor and lingering glances of the bashful maiden by his side.

Statues of George IV., William Pitt, Thomas Chalmers, and other prominent men have been erected on George Street, while at Charlotte Square a very fine equestrian figure of Prince Albert is situated. The design is quite elaborate, including paneled sides to the pedestal, with groups of working-men, sailors, children, and other persons carved upon it, who present flowers to the prince.

Melrose Abbey proved a place full of historic interest. This Rip Van Winkle village usually bears the name of the abbey in writing or printing its name, the ruin, in fact, constituting its chief attraction. A quiet restful atmosphere seems to pervade the place. Few people are astir. Marks of haste and bustle are happily absent.

> " If thou wouldst view fair Melrose aright,
> Go, visit it by the pale moonlight;

> For the gay beams of lightsome day
> Gild but to flout the ruins gray;
> When the broken arches are black in night,
> And each shafted oriel glimmers white;
> When the cold light's uncertain shower
> Streams on the ruin's central tower;
> When buttress and buttress alternately
> Seem framed of ebon and ivory;
> When silver edges the imagery,
> And the scrolls that teach thee to live and die;
> When distant Tweed is heard to rave,
> And the owlet to hoot o'er the dead man's grave;
> Then go—but go alone the while,
> Then view St. David's ruined pile;
> And, home returning, soothly swear
> Was never scene so sad and fair."

The crumbling walls of the abbey, overgrown with ivy and other traces of vegetable life, present, indeed, a mournful picture. A flock of jackdaws, disturbed by our presence, flew from their lonely nests in the crevices of the gray walls as we approached.

Founded by David I. in 1136, in the interest of the Cistercian Order of Monks, it was finally dedicated about ten years later. Fire and sword have since wrought terrible havoc with the beautiful and venerable structure. In 1322 Edward II. ruthlessly, in a spirit of absolute vandalism, robbed it of its sacred treasures, and the Church of St. Mary, identified with it, was burned. Subsequently, it was again rebuilt at the expense of Robert the Bruce. By the incendiary act of Richard II., in 1385, it was partially destroyed by fire. During the struggle of the Reformers its final ruin was achieved, and for more than two centuries the stones of which it was composed were carried away, and now form portions of many public and private buildings in the vicinity.

> "The moon on the east oriel shone,
> Through slender shafts of stately stone,
> By foliage-tracery combined;
> Thou wouldst have thought some fairy's hand,
> 'Twixt poplars straight, the ozier wand
> In many freakish knot had twined;
> Then framed a spell, when the work was done,
> And changed the willow wreath to stone."

Here the heroic and warlike Douglases slumber. William, Lord of Liddesdale, murdered during the reign of David I. while on a hunting expedition, was buried within its somber walls. The heart of Robert the Bruce was brought back from the bloody battle-field in Spain and here interred. On the day of our arrival a wreath of wild-flowers with some lines in writing rested over his buried heart. Some children on the previous Sabbath, from the fresh perusal of history, had made this tribute to his memory five hundred years after his death.

Nowhere in history could I recall so touching an instance of undying affection, save in the monumental and unparalleled tragedy of Calvary. The sacred Sufferer, notwithstanding the blatant infidelity of modern times and the lives of inconsistent professors, is still loved by numberless thousands, in all lands, between the rising and setting of the ruddy sun.

Michael Scott, the reputed wizard, was also buried within the inclosure. The following lines refer to the fact:

> "I buried him on St. Michael's night
> When the bell tolled one and the moon was bright:
> And I dug him a chamber among the dead
> When the floor of the chancel was stainèd red.
> That his patron's cross might over him wave
> And scare the fiends from the wizard's grave."

Sir Walter Scott came frequently from his mansion at Abbotsford, two and a half miles distant, when preparing certain of his works for the press, spending hours amid the impressive associations of the spot.

Local tradition asserts that William, Lord Soullis, was boiled alive in lead at the Nine-stane Rig, a well-known region not far distant from Melrose. The following lines relate to the statement:

> "And still beside the Nine-stane burn,
>   Ribbed like the sand at mark of sea,
> The ropes, that would not twist nor turn,
>   Shaped of the sifted sand you see.
> The black spae-book true Thomas he took:
>   Again its magic leaves he spread;
> And he found that to quell the powerful spell,
>   The wizard must be boiled in lead.

> On a circle of stones they placed the pot,
>   On a circle of stones but barely nine;
> They heated it red and fiery hot,
>   Till the burnished brass did glimmer and shine.
> They rolled him up in a sheet of lead,
>   A sheet of lead for a funeral pall;
> They plunged him in the caldron red,
>   And melted him, lead, and bones, and all."

Arriving at Abbotsford after a pleasant walk from the abbey, we found few visitors present, as the hour was comparatively early. The building is a substantial stone structure. Well-kept grounds, with a profusion of flowers and foliage, surround it. A few yards from the premises the Tweed goes murmuring by in its serpentine pathway to the sea. By a process of architectural evolution the house has grown since the period of its erection in 1811 by various additions, until its present ample proportions were reached in 1821 under Sir Walter's immediate supervision.

The interior is practically a museum, so numerous are the curiosities which accumulated during the lifetime of the distinguished author. Space can only be spared for the mention of a few of them.

The library, sixty by fifty feet, has a roof of carved oak, and contains nearly twenty thousand volumes, many of them being exceedingly rare and valuable. I was allowed to sit in the vacant arm-chair of the great writer as a special favor, a privilege seldom accorded to visitors, lest the leathern covering should wear out prematurely.

Among other curiosities were Highland broadswords, targets, matchlocks of the fifteenth century, bugle horns, and ancient instruments of torture; Rob Roy's gun; Napoleon I.'s pistol, found in his carriage after his flight from the overwhelming defeat at Waterloo; the hunting flask of James I., and the iron mask worn by George Wishart when he was burned at the stake.

Implements of warfare also exist, terrible souvenirs of the dark period, when

> "Ancrum Moor
> Ran red with English blood;
> Where the Douglas true, and the bold Buccleuch,
> 'Gainst keen Lord Evers stood."

There are also two elbow-chairs, the gift of Pope Pius, an ebony writing-desk presented by George III., and a silver urn sent by Lord Byron from Greece. The garments last worn by the illustrious and indefatigable writer are also shown, consisting of the plaid trowsers, striped vest, blue coat, a broad brimmed white hat, and a pair of well brushed walking-shoes. By them lies his walking-stick—one of a dozen or more collected by him. New canes were frequently selected by Sir Walter during his numerous rambles in the forest. The guide described him as a bad shot, but observed that he excelled as a fisherman, in reply to an interrogation from me.

A large chest strongly bound with metal bands was also shown, which, it was soberly declared, was the identical one in which the bride playfully hid herself at the famous wedding-feast—and, the spring-lock preventing her escape, it became her coffin. Since then the tale has been told in many forms, alike in poetry and prose, with, of course, many fanciful additions, though the story is based upon sober fact. The chest is said to have been subsequently presented to Sir Walter, who was a well-known antiquarian.

His remains rest at Dryburgh Abbey. The massive granite shaft bears the simple inscription, "Sir Walter Scott, Baronet, died September 21st, 1832." By his side sleep his wife, his son, Lieutenant-Colonel Scott, who died at sea, and Lockhart, his son-in-law.

> "So there in solemn solitude,
>   In that sequestered spot,
> Lies mingled with its kindred clay
>   The dust of Walter Scott!
> The glowing dreams of bright romance
>   That, teeming, filled his ample brow;
> Where is his daring chivalry?
>   Where are his visions now?
>
> The flashing eye is dimmed for aye;
>   The stalwart limb is stiff and cold;
> No longer pours his trumpet note
>   To wake the jousts of old!

> The generous heart, the open hand,
>   The ruddy cheek, the silver hair,
> Are moldering in the silent dust—
>   All, all is lonely there."

An additional walk from the mansion of a mile over a smooth road, between neatly trimmed hedgerows, brought me to the banks of the bonny Tweed. No bridge was found; but a rowboat did good service and conveyed me to the opposite shore, the oars being vigorously plied by the ferry-woman, who received one penny (two cents) from each passenger, with which she was quite content. As no hotel or village was found, here and there a house being the only indication of civilized life, I managed to secure a lunch at one of them, and after waiting two hours took a very slow train, which, after many delays, brought me to my hotel in Edinburgh.

Glasgow was passing through a rainy period at the time of my visit. As elsewhere, however, no time was wasted in consequence of bad weather. The stone buildings, darkened by smoke and age, seemed almost black during wet weather. Nearly all Scottish buildings are constructed of stone from native quarries. Durability and a wearisome sameness are the impressions made by them on the mind of the traveler.

This city traces its origin to St. Mungo, who built a cell near the spot in 539 A. D. His followers, who listened to his preaching, finally constituted him a bishop and king, and the nucleus of the great city of Glasgow existed.

George Square contains several fine statues of distinguished personages; Queen Victoria, Livingstone, James Watt, Sir Walter Scott, Sir John Moore, Lord Clyde, Thomas Campbell, Prince Albert, Thomas Graham, Robert Burns, Sir Robert Peel, and James Oswald being thus honored.

On Queen Street stands a fine equestrian statue of Wellington with paneled sides, giving spirited and well-executed views of his principal engagements. Kelingrove Park, beautifully laid out, looked fresh and inviting, owing to recent rains, and displayed fountains. The park contains choice landscape views and several pieces of statuary, one in memory of Robert Stewart, through whose instrumentality the excellent system of water supply was introduced into this manufacturing city. From the park hill a superb view of that portion of the city is afforded. It appeared to be the Fifth Avenue section of the city, so to speak. Two large cannon captured at Sebastopol occupy a conspicuous position at the summit.

Glasgow is entitled to the honor of launching the first steamer built in Europe, in 1812. James Watt was a native of this city, and as early as 1763 successfully applied steam as a motive power. On the

Clyde I counted between fifty and sixty iron and steel steamers of various dimensions and stages of progress in process of construction. The United States, as well as other nations, in view of the regulations respecting tariff and other causes, find it much more profitable to procure their ships in a foreign market than at home.

A radical defect exists somewhere in our theory of political economy, which successfully drives American shipping merchants to Great Britain, where hundreds of iron steam-ships are constructed, which, under a more statesmanlike policy, would be manufactured by our own skillful and deserving mechanics.

On the steamer *Madge Wildfire* I sailed for the "Land o' Burns and Tam O'Shanter." Many charming villages dotted the banks of the Clyde as we sped along, including Greenock, Androssan, and Rothesay. Several of them derive their chief importance from the excellent sea-beaches that exist, which, with summer hotels, attract many visitors, from various points in Great Britain especially.

The day for the season was cold and cheerless, and a drizzling rain fell much of the time. At Ayr we arrived at length, but a drive of nearly three miles to the Burns cottage and monument remained. The latter was erected in 1820 at a cost of $17,000. It is situated within an acre of well-kept ground near the old cottage and kirk. From the top of the monument a good view of the adjacent country is furnished, each object suggesting some stirring lines from the writings of the farmer poet. The well where

"Mungo's mither hanged hersel,"

and in another direction the tourist can descry quite clearly

"Alloway's auld haunted kirk."

At the cottage, bearing the inscription, "Robert Burns, born January 25, 1759; died July 21, 1796," the bed on which Burns was born is exhibited, together with many other objects of interest. Souvenirs on sale in the house were eagerly purchased by visitors, and after a lunch, furnished in the same building, the "auld kirk" was visited, which the poet attended when a boy. It is a ruin, a mere shell, the walls only remaining. Old graves in the neglected yard surrounding the church were scrutinized, including that of Burns's father. Wearisome guides who reel off yards of Burns's poetry unbidden in a barbarous dialect, and inflict apocryphal stories on the miserable listener in ardent hopes of gain, are politely snubbed.

But the hour for return has arrived. We must not miss our steamer. Had time afforded we should have called at the residence of Burns's niece, who resides in the neighborhood. So away we dash at a rapid rate in our well-filled omnibus over a most excellent road, across the "brig o' Doon," and arrive in good season at the steam-boat landing at Ayr.

On the way the Wallace tower, erected on the site of his imprisonment, is pointed out. It is a handsome Gothic shaft, built in 1835, and is one hundred and fifteen feet in height. The old tavern which Burns frequented still stands. Alas! his convivial habits cut short a promising and extraordinary career at the early age of thirty-six. His description of Nancy, and their blind and mutual infatuation for each other, a verse of which is quoted, might also be applied to the seductive and deadly fumes of the bottle. An undercurrent of religious sentiment was ever and anon disclosing itself, however, in his nature and writings, as the "Cotter's Saturday Night," and several other poems abundantly show.

> "I'll ne'er blame my partial fancy—
> Naething could resist my Nancy;
> But to see her was to love her,
> Love but her and love forever.
> Had we never loved sae kindly,
> Had we never loved sae blindly,
> Never met or never parted,
> We had ne'er been broken hearted."

It was night when the *Madge Wildfire* landed us at the bridge quay of Glasgow.

CHAPTER V.

THE BELFAST RIOTS.—IRELAND'S LARGEST LAKE.—CONCERNING CROWS.—BATTLE OF THE BOYNE.—JAUNTING-CAR RIDES.—DUBLIN AND ITS SIGHTS.—SIEGE OF DERRY, 1689.—GIANTS' CAUSEWAY.

> "Let Erin remember the days of old,
>   Ere her faithless sons betray'd her;
> When Malachi wore the collar of gold
>   Which he won from her proud invader;
> When her kings with standard of green unfurl'd
>   Led the Red Branch Knight to danger;
> Ere the emerald gem of the western world
>   Was set in the crown of a stranger.
>
> "On Lough Neagh's bank as the fisherman strays,
>   When the clear cold eve's declining,
> He sees the round tower of other days
>   In the wave beneath him shining;
> Thus shall memory often in dreams sublime
>   Catch a glimpse of the days that are over;
> Thus sighing look through the waves of time
>   For the long faded glories they cover."

ON my arrival at Belfast, after a rough passage on a Scotch steamer from Glasgow, the streets of that enterprising and attractive city were stained with the red blood of many of her citizens. For several weeks the deplorable internecine struggle had continued, with occasional lulls in the war of religionists —Protestant and Catholic. Many points of the city were occupied by the military, especially centers of the riotous population. Weak and "goody-goody" proclamations from the civil authorities appeared in the public press, calculated from their inherent imbecility to stimulate rather than repress disorder. But little better, if any, were the editorials of leading journals. The mob had terrorized the entire region of country, and knew it. Many shopkeepers, fearing the loss of trade, the destruction of their property, or in downright cowardice, were suspected of furnishing moral aid at least to the rioters. Mistaken and fatal policy! Country buyers were conspicuous by their absence. Tourists by scores who had secured rooms at hotels and elsewhere countermanded their orders. The summer, which ordinarily produces a rich financial harvest, was worse than wasted. Fears of famine and terrible suffering on the part of the poor during the approaching winter were freely expressed by many thoughtful citizens.

The "island men," as they were styled, ship carpenters and other working-men, went strongly guarded by the military and constabulary to their daily toil. Crowds, about equally composed of friends and foes, witnessed their return to their families at nightfall. Spies in citizens' clothing from the police office, and also the mob, dogged my steps in various portions of Belfast. Other tourists observed that they were watched also, while some were warned to keep within doors or prudently depart by an early train.

What is the disturbance about? Nothing! The bad blood which culminated in the battle of the Boyne in 1690 still exists. The brilliant victory of William, Prince of Orange, and the disastrous defeat of the army led by James II.—a poor general and a consummate coward—settled nothing. An annual crop of "Orange riots" has been the unhappy fruit of that bloody contest on July 12, its anniversary, in many lands since that period.

Fitz John Porter's theory of throttling a riot at the outset, even at the cost of lives, has apparently not reached Ireland. A few experienced American detectives to ferret out the ringleaders and bring them to swift punishment might prove quite useful also. Had Inspector Williams and the New York police force been on duty in Belfast at the inception of the fresh disturbances that summer, the miserable battle of "Kilkenny cats" would have been stamped out in twenty-four hours.

Belfast presents comparatively few points of interest to the average tourist. Its broad and well cleaned streets, public buildings, and charming private residences of the "well-to-do" portion of the population convey a pleasing aspect, however. The Albert Memorial Tower, with its huge clock having

THATCHED COTTAGE, IRELAND.

four dials, one on each side, stands in an open plaza and is regarded with much local pride by citizens. Situated on the river Lagan, at the very head of Belfast Lough, with a harbor adapted to the capacity of a medium class of ocean steamers, the city is the commercial center of the Province of Ulster. It is distant from Dublin eighty-eight miles. The population, owing to the emigration to America and the war of conflicting sects, constantly fluctuates, seldom rising above one hundred thousand. A substantial stone bridge crosses the Lagan, near which the shipping quays are situated. Its industries include ship-building, foundries, vitriol works, tan-yards, flour-mills, distilleries, breweries, and the manufacture of rope, felt, cotton, and linen goods. Steamers sail regularly for London, Liverpool, Dublin, Glasgow, and many other ports in Great Britain. Queen's College stands at the head of its educational institutions, and for many years has received an appropriation of £7,000 for its maintenance. Several railways extend from the city to various parts of the island, and "home rule" of a character that will restore harmony among her people is all that is required to enhance her future prosperity.

Lough Neagh, the largest lake in Ireland, I saw from a point near Antrim, a quiet and secluded spot. My position was not well chosen, I learned later.

Though the broad expanse of water, with great white waves tossing in their wild grandeur before the brisk morning breeze, was distinctly visible, still it was remote from any human habitation. No dock or boats were in sight. A few men were adjusting their fishing-nets preparatory for future uses. A company of young men strolled through the adjacent woodland that fringed the shore, while the inevitable crow, so prevalent and unmolested in England, Ireland, and Scotland, gave a few dismal caws and flapped his dusky wings over my head. Strangely enough, the crow, the victim of scarecrows, poison, and shotguns at the hands of the American farmer, is allowed to "be fruitful and multiply" indefinitely by the agriculturist of Great Britain. His longevity is due to the prevailing impression that his diet consists of worms and bugs rather than grain.

At Drogheda I left the train to visit the famous battle-field of the Boyne. Securing a jaunting-car at the railway station, with a good-natured and communicative driver, we started for the historic spot, some three miles or more distant. Much of the way, after leaving the ancient place, with its grim stone walls and narrow streets, the road ran through a pleasant farming region situated on the beautiful banks of the Boyne. The position held by the troops of James II. in the memorable battle was pointed out, and certainly it was a strong one—in fact, a miniature Gibraltar. About thirty thousand troops were engaged on each side. Long before the battle was over, according to Kohl, King James fled precipitately from the field. By a forced ride he reached Dublin Castle in a few hours. Here he complained to Lady Tyr-

AN IRISH HOTEL.

connel that her countrymen, the Irish, were cowards—would run well, but not fight. With keen native wit, which cut like a Damascus blade, she sarcastically replied, while her eyes flashed fire :

"In this, as in every thing else, Your Majesty surpasses them, for you have won the race." The next day the king, anxious for his personal safety, continued his flight on horseback, reaching Waterford at nightfall, one hundred miles distant from Dublin. At length he arrived in France, where he died of apoplexy eleven years subsequently, aged sixty-eight. Bearing the title of William III., the Prince of Orange jointly assumed the throne with Mary, his wife, and the righteous reign of William and Mary began.

A tasteful monument situated on a knoll, erected in 1736, commemorates the victory achieved by the forces successfully led by William, who was the son-in-law of the defeated and deposed monarch.

Dundalk, fifty-eight miles from Belfast, on the line of the Great Northern Railway leading to Dublin, is a prominent manufacturing town. It derives its chief importance, however, in the history of Ireland as the place where the coronation of successive kings has taken place. Here Edward Bruce was crowned King of Ireland. In an engagement with the English two years afterward he fell mortally wounded.

Dublin, the capital, is replete with objects of interest and historical associations. The castle, the official residence of the lord lieutenant, may be regarded as the "head center," to borrow the language of the Fenian. For a sixpence the doors of the state apartments swung open before us, with a young lady as guide. She counseled the visitors to "walk on the Holland" that had been spread to preserve the carpets, which direction we faithfully complied with. Paintings representing a long line of lord lieutenants stretching through very many years adorned the walls of the spacious suite of rooms, together with works of art of a miscellaneous character. The furniture, costly and durable, was well covered to protect it from dust and wear.

Another sixpence admitted us to the Chapel Royal, where the lord lieutenant, his family, and a few other persons have private services on the Sabbath. How potent is money! All doors except those of heaven open before it. I reminded some of the prominent citizens that the Great Teacher did not conduct services under lock and key, but on the green, grassy sward, and by the sacred and solemn sea-shore of Galilee; that he "ate with publicans and sinners," "the common people hearing him gladly." How strange to us a private chapel for the President of the United States would seem. The chapel is composed of richly carved oak, and is a gem of beauty.

On another occasion, in company with a government clerk, I was permitted to visit the beautiful grounds connected with the private residence of the lord lieutenant at Phœnix Park. The scene of the brutal and cowardly murders of Lord Cavendish and Burke was pointed out. Visitors on foot and by carriage came to the spot every few moments. A volunteer guide described the tragedy to as many as cared to listen to him, and eagerly clutched the proffered pence and halfpennies which were extended to him. An apple, cake, and lemonade woman did a small business in the sale of refreshments to the sight-seers who gathered.

The extent of the park surprised me. Much of it is left in its primitive wildness, with but slight changes made by the landscape gardener. Wellington's monument (himself an Irishman), on the same grounds, is an immense granite shaft, in form reminding one faintly of the pyramids. It is a curious fact that Wellington was born at Dublin the same year that Napoleon was born at Corsica. The chief victories of the great warrior are inscribed upon the column. Not far distant stands the equestrian statue of Lord Gough in recognition of his important military achievements.

At the head-quarters of the constabulary a police drill was in progress to sweet music from the Dublin band, pronounced by my guide the best musicians in Ireland. About seventy-five raw recruits in citizens' dress, undeterred by the broken heads of the Belfast police force at the hands of an infuriated mob, were eagerly undergoing a military drill, expecting soon to be blended permanently with the men in actual service.

In other portions of the city some very fine statues of several of the eminent sons of Ireland were observed. The O'Connell monument; Nelson's column; with fine statues of O'Brien, Goldsmith, Moore, Grattan, and an equestrian figure of George IV. in a curious costume, the latter having the appearance of a hunted Modoc fleeing for life before the swift horses of the United States cavalry.

The discussion over the question of "home rule," temporarily defeated, at least at the polls, promises to evoke a prolonged and bitter contest. Since nearly one half of the voting population has expressed a desire for the resuscitation of the home Parliament at Dublin, I was anxious to visit the old Parliament buildings still standing. They are in excellent repair, now being occupied by the Bank of Ireland. The House of Commons is used as the counting-room, while the House of Lords serves the purpose of a bank parlor. The magic English sixpence took me through the building, with a bank porter as a guide, who not only furnished me with some valuable information, but actually allowed me to take an unchallenged seat in the House of Lords! No material change has been made in the latter room since the final dissolution of the Irish Parliament and the union of Ireland with Great Britain in 1801.

As an illustration of the low wages paid in Ireland

to a certain class of clerks I would mention those received by a young lady in charge of a railway refreshment counter in Dublin. Learning that I was an American, she was anxious to glean information regarding our country, including the wages received in various avocations. Her salary was, she informed me, but twelve pounds per annum, including her meals at the restaurant. Out of this she must pay for her lodgings, dress well, and be on duty from half past four A. M. until midnight. If the salaries in other departments of labor are proportionately low it is not surprising that thousands continue to sail for the American continent as a veritable " **Land of Promise.**"

A day was spent at Kingstown, Bray, and Killiney, in the suburbs of Dublin. They serve the purposes of Long Branch and Newport during the summer season, affording the people of the Irish metropolis an opportunity to enjoy a sniff of the sea air or a salt-water bath at a moderate expense. From Mt. Mapas, in the village of Killiney, I secured a superb and never-to-be-forgotten view of the entire region of country. The monument on its summit and the substantial walls inclosing the grounds were paid for by Sir John Mapas, during a year of severity, to furnish employment for the suffering and starving poor in the vicinity. Mountains, valleys, well-tilled farms, the winding pathway of the railway, which at last lost itself in a tunnel in the mountain like a snake that has found its hole, were traceable. The expansive waters of St. George's Channel and the Irish Sea, dotted here and there by the smoke of a distant steamer, or bearing on their glassy bosoms sailing vessels of different dimensions, whose snowy sails seemed like the wings of the dove conveying the seamen and officers to their destined haven, constituted a delightful spectacle.

Much to my regret I was compelled to omit my contemplated visit to Cork and Blarney Castle, in its vicinity, owing to a lack of time. According to the familiar tradition, whosoever visits the "Groves of Blarney" and imprints a kiss upon the "Blarney-stone" thenceforward becomes wonderfully eloquent and fascinating in speech. Or, as the song goes,

> "There is a stone there
> That whoever kisses,
> O, he never misses
> To grow eloquent;
> 'Tis he may clamber
> To a lady's chamber,
> Or become a member
> Of Parliament.
> A clever spouter
> He'll sure turn out, or
> An out and outer

>   To be let alone!
>   Don't hope to hinder him,
>   Sure he's a pilgrim
>   From the 'Blarney-stone.'"

Of course such extraordinary powers would not be bad to have. How serviceable for the political stump orator, or when collecting bad debts, or in settling disputed claims and overcharges with one's landlord at his hotel or with the omnipresent hackman, or in adjusting a heated domestic dispute with one's mother-in-law. Still, self-denial must be practiced. It would not do for some people to receive all the good things of earth. So I compromised the matter and bestowed several ardent kisses on the rugged rocks of Mt. Mapas, which, after all, may serve me quite as well as the "Blarney-stone."

A tram, or street-car, as we style it in America, brought me to the famous Donnybrook fair-grounds in the outskirts of Dublin. No exhibition has been given there for a period of twenty-five years. Buildings will soon cover the original site. The Donnybrook church (Catholic) stands near the premises with its doors hospitably open, as is customary with that denomination, welcoming alike the Protestant or one of their own faith. Let the day soon dawn when the doors of our own faith shall also be swung open in a similar manner!

What crowds once attended the fair, which lasted a week or more! People from remote parts of the island and from near by; men in broadcloth and corduroy, in new garments and in rags; women in homespun linen, and others in silks and satins; sheep, cattle, goats, pigs, fruit, vegetables, and a thousand other attractions. What warm greetings on the part of old friends! And, alas! occasionally at least, what vigorous combats with the shillalah when the passions were fired with whisky. How calm the green fields seem now, like the smooth smiling sea when the tempest has subsided!

The Sabbath spent in Dublin was quiet and restful. At a Church of Ireland service (the Magdalen) in the morning I found a good-sized congregation, and listened to a thoughtful discourse. In the evening I saw a small congregation, about seventy-five in all, at the Rutland Square Presbyterian Church. A good sermon, plain and practical, was given. The choir sang each psalm at such a rapid rate that even when the tunes were familiar it was quite difficult to keep company with them. No organ or instrumental music of any kind were used during the service. Dr. John Hall was pastor of this church previous to his acceptance of a $10,000 call in gold from his present parish at Fifth Avenue, New York.

Fewer tourists have visited Ireland the present

season (1889) than formerly. The riotous proceedings which have occurred in portions of the country are some of the chief causes, as already stated. A driver of a jaunting-car, as he took me on my journey, deeply deplored the hard times in his calling.

"No business is being done," he continued; "and you," he said in conclusion, "are about the only gentleman in the place."

I did not construe this to be a personal compliment, but, on the contrary, inferred that it was a local term, implying a tourist, or a person with money to spend, traveling for pleasure. How multitudes of people in Ireland subsist is an unsolved problem, even in the summer season. During the winter the gaunt wolf of hunger and absolute want must make miserable many a humble home. As in all great cities the world over, Dublin has its streets of downright wretchedness, poverty, and crime. A few paltry pence derived from some unknown source must keep them alive somehow. Many struggle for years to accumulate sufficient funds to secure a steerage passage to America. Scarcely a family with whom I conversed but hoped to hear through me from friends in the United States. Often they could not tell where they were located. One poor peasant was anxious to hear from a relative in "Rockford," but could not tell in what State it was. He was surprised when I told him that there probably was a score of places bearing the same name in the Union.

Londonderry is a city of ancient origin. It is situated on an oval-shaped hill, the ancient wall with four gates remaining, though the place has grown immensely beyond the original barriers. Derry is the name by which it was first known, and the one most frequently used in business circles to-day. The prefix "London" dates from the time of James II., who granted charters to twelve London companies after the rebellion at that period had been subdued.

At the beginning of the siege of 1689, while the citizens had nearly lost their heads at the approach of King James's troops under Lord Antrim, several apprentice boys, with rare presence of mind, closed the gates of the city against the invaders. A terrible siege of one hundred and five days ensued. So hard were the inhabitants pressed for provisions that dogs and rats were eagerly devoured, more than two thousand persons perishing in the awful struggle.

In commemoration of the noble action of the apprentice boys the event is duly celebrated with an "apprentices' holiday" once a year. The general commanding during the siege, who favored surrendering the city to the foe, is then burned in effigy. A fine structure, known as the "Apprentice Boys' Hall," has also been erected, besides a fine Doric column on which is a statue of the Rev. George Walker, who assisted in the defense of the city with great courage and stimulated the drooping spirits of the brave and patriotic citizens. The river Foyle divides the place. A substantial bridge crosses the broad and beautiful stream to the opposite shore, which is still styled Waterside, though embraced within the city limits. Our route to the Giants' Causeway led through the picturesque villages of Coleraine, Portrush, and in full view of Dunluce Castle and the borders of the great Atlantic. The castle exhibits its outer walls and general outlines only. What traditions and historic tales linger around the spot!—love, marriage, hate, war, the rise and fall of conflicting clans. How full of suggestive points to the poet, novelist, and play-writer!

At Portrush an excellent and imposing monument to the memory of the celebrated Dr. Adam Clarke, the industrious, scholarly, and profound Wesleyan commentator, was erected in 1859. Funds for the cause were contributed by his admirers in the United States and Great Britain. At Port Stewart a memorial building was also erected in recognition of his services to the Christian world, which is used as a church and school-house. Dr. Clarke died of cholera, August 26, 1832.

The "Giants' Causeway" formed a fitting and sublime climax to my devious and weary wanderings in Ireland, not to speak of many other lands. Nature is here presented in some of its wildest and almost inex-

CLARKE'S MONUMENT, PORTRUSH.

plicable aspects. The caverns into which gigantic waves, seething and foaming, dash with relentless fury when the tide is rising, the basaltic columns stretching a thousand feet or more out, out, until lost in the deep blue sea, are alike objects of vast interest. Then there is the stone and arched gateway, looking like the work of mortals; the organ, as forms resembling organ-pipes on the sides of the cliff are called; the columns themselves, cut as if by square, compass, and chisel, with regular sides, varying capriciously. They included the quadrangle, heptagon, octagon, and possibly other forms in the strange aggregation.

But few tourists were present, since the season was well advanced and the morning positively cold. We stood in the bleak wind that swept down upon us from the sea. An army of guides, hotel runners, peddlers, and beggars, regarding us as their lawful prey, descended on our party in full force, like a swarm of mosquitoes around a belated traveler in a gloomy swamp. Following my guide, as the water was too rough for the use of rowboats, I was led to the edge of the precipice where the "Shepherd's Path" would lead us to the prominent points of interest. After following him for a time down the dizzy heights, almost perpendicular, I gave up in despair. Hanging over the awful abyss by the ends of my fingers, with an inch of stone for one foot and the other on nothing, it was a critical moment. Weighing nearly two hundred pounds, I could not long endure the unusual and terrible strain. My strength was failing. The probability of being dashed to pieces on the rocks one hundred feet below was manifest. Home was three thousand five hundred miles away. Encouraged by the guide, I at last rested one foot in his hand and slid down to a better foothold in comparative safety. An hour of careful walking along the front of a frightful precipice in a goat's path, without a bush or support of any kind to prevent my fall. All things finally end, and so did the descent. When I reached the bottom I was utterly worn out; my clothing much the worse for the trip. I dared hardly look at the wild waves at the base of the cliff coming down lest dizziness should cause me to fall. All points of the Causeway were carefully examined, however, but the perils of that unhappy hour are ineffaceably engraven on my memory. Owing to the severe muscular strain and nervous shock I was so lame and exhausted for several days that exertion proved an absolute torture.

According to Rev. John Hall, D.D., himself a distinguished and widely known native of the "Emerald Isle," Sligo possesses great natural attractions, and is graphically described as follows: "County Sligo is naturally picturesque with 'mountain, stream, and sea,' and its county town, Sligo, with nearly eleven thousand people, and the capital of the north-west, is in a most striking and beautiful position. It lies in a valley up to which, through smooth green islands, stretches modestly an arm of the sea. On one side, a few miles off, the grand mountain, Knocknaroe, and on the other Benbulbin, tower aloft, and both slope down gracefully to the water's edge. Following them backward the eye traces range after range of graceful form, with space for fertile valleys between. No other town is known to me with surroundings more impressive.

"The harbor admits steamers big enough to go to Liverpool and Glasgow once a week. Just now an American steamer with three thousand tons of corn is lying at the entrance, tenders carrying her cargo into the town. The channel ought to grow deeper to receive such visitors. But what alterations have forty years made in the place? To begin with, the dress of the people has changed. The old frieze, by which a Connaught man used to be known, has given place to common cloth, and the fancy varieties, such as tennis players affect, are common.

"The women favor flowers on their hats. Many girls and women wear what used to be counted boys' caps. The heels of their boots have gained in depth what they have lost in breadth. All the cheaper ornamentation abounds, including chains that look like gold, and stones that are not very precious. A number of the houses have been improved and public buildings have advanced notably. But, alas! the town, as a whole, is not bigger nor busier than forty years ago. A common working-man earns about three dollars a week, but his house costs him fifty cents, and he has generally a numerous family. Yet Sligo is the port of supply and of export for much of a province. A handsome court-house and a showy town hall adorn the place.

"The Roman Catholics are ten to one Protestant, and a fine cathedral, which is said to have cost £50,000, with a palace for the bishop on a corresponding scale, rather astonishes a visitor, for within fifty yards of them are rows of thatched cottages. On a similar plan are church edifices and 'presbyteries'—as they call parsonages—being constructed all over the poorest parts of the land. A member of the denomination criticised the plan severely in talking with me, in ignorance of my views: ' 'Twould be a power betther, sure, if they tried to raise the people.'

"The surprising number of lame, deformed, and broken-down people around the streets surprised me, and to a question on the subject put to an intelligent man the reply was given: 'Yes; this is the sort that stays at home; the strong ones go to Ameriky, and the money that supports many of these comes from them.' Describing, as he did clearly, the small farms, say, of three or four acres, and twice that number of children on them, the question was put, 'Would it make them comfortable if they owned the three or four acres and paid no rent?' 'Not a bit of it, sur; what they want is trade, same as they have in Belfast or in Liverpool.' Why it does not come he could not tell. The most pushing traders in these western little towns are commonly Northmen or Scotchmen. Something more is needed than mere law can do. The girl who got a love-letter done by a type-writer, and who answered that she could not be 'courted by machinery,' is typical of communities. They cannot be lifted by mere acts of Parliament."

Long might we linger among this warm-hearted and mirth-loving people! Her valleys of verdure, placid lakes, and lonely glens prove an unfailing source of delight.

Farewell, lovely Ireland, farewell! With your mountains of green, valleys of fertility, generous hearts, and hospitable homes I bid you long farewell. May peace and prosperity characterize your future and cause the "Emerald Isle" to "blossom as the rose."

Each country has charms peculiarly its own. Even though crushed by the iron heel of despotism, or if it be simply a sterile waste amid the awful solitudes of the North Pole or within the dismal desolation of Terra del Fuego, some are found who apply to it the magic and endearing appellation of home.

CHAPTER VI.

OFF FOR PARIS.—A DISMAL NIGHT JOURNEY.—THE GAY METROPOLIS.—FALL OF THE BASTILE.—THE EXPOSITION OF 1889.—A CONTINENTAL SUNDAY.

"It is my wish that my ashes may repose on the banks of the Seine, in the midst of the French people, whom I have loved so well."—*Extract from Napoleon's Will.*

"*Aujourd' hui roi, demain rien*" (To-day a king, to-morrow nothing).

ON my first visit to Paris, 1886, I departed from London by a night excursion train, which had been extensively advertised, to avail myself of the reduced rates. How I regretted the act a few hours later! Deprived of the always pleasing view of the charming English landscapes, its profusion of hedgerows and attractive villages on the journey, an unfailing source of delight to me on previous trips, additional trials awaited us. The night for the season was intensely cold on the steamer plying between Dover and Calais. No shelter was furnished from the strong wind which blew fore and aft with considerable violence; the seats were all occupied by passengers, while the water was rough. At half past one A. M. we finally landed, and learned that the excursion train would not start for Paris, two hundred and twenty-five miles distant, until five o'clock. So the remainder of the night was spent miserably enough in the dirty, dimly lighted, and sepulchral railway station.

In the gray dawn of the morning, glad to emerge from the doleful den, I strolled through the quaint and sleeping city. The footfall of a drowsy policeman or the rumbling wheels of approaching market-wagons alone broke the silence. The antique buildings—monuments commemorative of the military struggle of 1558, when it was captured from the English by Francis, Duke of Guise, after being under British rule for a period of two hundred years—attracted attention, together with its strong and massive fortifications.

Paris was reached at ten o'clock. The bustling and mercurial city of pleasure and fashion was in a state of unwonted excitement. A national *fête* day was approaching. The armies of France were to contribute thirty-five thousand soldiers for the occasion. From all public buildings, shops, *cafés*, and thousands of private residences the national colors floated in great profusion. Preliminary indications of the coming event in the sporadic discharge of firearms and cannon-crackers in various portions of the gay city were manifest. I was privileged to witness the grand military review when the day finally came. Paris was wild with excitement. All street-cars, or "trams," as they are called in Europe, leading to the beautiful park, Long Champs, were crowded. An army of civilians came also on foot and in carriages. A vast sea of French were at last crowded together —soldiers and citizens. A flood of rain fell a few moments after the various columns were in motion. It was endured patiently for a season by the populace, but shelter was soon sought under the adjacent trees. The soldiers, of course, patiently submitted to the drenching. Water was fearlessly faced then, even if France quailed at *Water*-loo. Excellent marching by the mighty army with delightful music from the numerous bands were furnished. The latter were entirely too near each other, producing at times marked discord. Soon the rain disappeared, and when night came Paris was in a blaze of splendor. Electric and colored lights flashed every-where. Many public buildings were brilliantly illuminated. The theaters and ball-rooms were thronged, while thousands of well-dressed pedestrians crowded the streets until a very late hour.

While the review was in progress I thought of the Franco-Prussian War, with the complete and terrible overthrow of Napoleon III. and his plans, his death, and later the sad end of his only son by the hand of a barbarous warrior in a distant land. The various regiments were composed chiefly of young men, the majority of them being small in stature.

The tomb of Napoleon at the Hotel des Invalides was surrounded by a throng of sight-seers on the day of my visit. Here the great warrior slumbers. The victor in fifty battles; alas! the man of blood.

> "He sleeps his last sleep, he has fought his last battle;
> No sound can awake him to glory again."

Several of his mighty generals repose near him in the same structure.

An extract from the will of Napoleon in French is inscribed over the doorway of the crypt. The following is a translation: "It is my wish that my ashes may repose on the banks of the Seine, in the midst of the French people, whom I have loved so well."

The hat and sword worn by Napoleon at Austerlitz are here on exhibition. At Des Invalides other relics of the emperor are found in this military museum and home of aged and crippled soldiers.

As customary with tourists, the Church of Notre Dame, the Tuileries, the Palais de L'Industrie, the July Column on the site of the infernal Bastile, the boulevards, and other points of interest in the great city were duly visited. Sails on the little steamers of the Seine, with winds through the prominent portions of the city, furnished needed rest from the severer labors of sight-seeing, though in another channel.

According to a modern and competent writer, "The Bastile was at first a fortress and then a gloomy prison, and probably looked like one of the sugar

LOUVRE IN THE SIXTEENTH CENTURY.

refineries on the banks of the East River, Brooklyn, N. Y. It was built in 1369, when Charles V. was king, and was enlarged and improved by his successors. There is a tradition, probably untrue, that its builder, Hugues Aubriot, was the first prisoner to be confined in it.

"The walls of the Bastile were thirty or forty feet thick at the base and twelve feet thick in the upper towers. It was surrounded by a dry ditch twenty-five feet deep, which was defended by a high wall. The building was impregnable to any artillery of the time of the French Revolution.

"The prisoners were confined in the eight towers, and they looked on the outer world through twelve feet of masonry and a triple row of bars. If the prisoner was sentenced to severer confinement he was put in a dungeon nineteen feet below the level of the court-yard and five feet below the level of the ditch. Here, to the man buried alive, a slender shaft of light came through a narrow loophole communicating with the ditch.

"From being a fortress the Bastile gradually became a national prison for prisoners of state. The French peasants, tradesmen, and artisans were not confined there, but the prisoners were men of consequence, many of them being conspirators against the king. Among the famous prisoners who have been caged in the Bastile are 'The Man in the Iron Mask,' Voltaire, Cardinal Rohan, De Latude, and Marshal Richelieu.

"Important prisoners were often kept in solitary confinement, but most of them were allowed considerable freedom. They could take exercise in the court-yard and indulge in games.

"The state provided well for their support, but they were often miserably fed, owing to the stealing of their allowance by the prison officials. The great cruelty of the Bastile was that an innocent man might be sent there through the malice and power of a private enemy, and live and die there, forgotten by the world.

"In the time of Louis XVI. the Bastile had degenerated into a common jail. When it was surrendered to the storming revolutionists of Paris, more than one hundred years ago, there were only seven prisoners in it. Yet one, the Count de Solage, had been a prisoner since his eleventh year, and another, Tavernier, had been thirty years in the Bastile, and was dazed by his release.

"More than ten thousand Frenchmen captured the Bastile from its little garrison, and then they cut off the governor's head and carried it on a pike. The Bastile was torn down, and on its site stands the bronze Column of July."

Fragments of French derived from my early studies and four visits to Canada were, I soon discovered, of little value to me. The accent of Parisian French is peculiar. Much depends on the expression of the countenance and the inevitable shrug of the shoulder also, so characteristic of the natives.

Sunday in Paris is violated in a manner that is positively shocking to a New Englander, if not to the average American. No one can fully comprehend the meaning of the term "Continental Sunday" until he has visited Paris and Brussels at least.

The sidewalks in front of the principal *cafés* are crowded with little iron tables to the curb-stone, where men, women, and children sip wine, drink beer, and eat. In some instances two or three rows of tables are placed in the roadway among the vehicles when those on the sidewalks are occupied. Military processions with bands of music are common. Hand-organs are heard ever and anon, while the inevitable monkey solicits centimes from the public for the benefit of his lynx-eyed master. Theaters are open, small shows with wheels of fortune and other games of chance line the sidewalk, while peddlers and distributors of circulars are common, and with shops generally open, constitute portions of the sad picture.

Our second trip to the city of fashion and spectacular display was also by night. Though the waters of the English Channel for once were sufficiently quiet, yet the steamer was over-crowded. On double rows of bunks placed around the dining-table in the cabin passengers lay side by side. Strangers were the companions of the fortunate ones finding beds; the feet of one row nearing the heads of those in the next. Hundreds found no resting-place at all, like

Noah's dove in its preliminary flight. They walked the deck, counted the stars, watched wistfully for the faintest suggestion of the French coast at Dieppe, or drank and ate at the cabin table, and paid roundly for their temerity. Obviously, those having berths could find no sleep amid the rattle of dishes, murmur of many voices, and the lights that flashed in their faces. There was no moon and absolutely no light on the upper deck, and but one or two dim lamps on the main deck. At three o'clock in the morning all were obliged to grope their way through the darkness down the narrow gang-plank to the pier, giving up their tickets at the same time. As each one carried some articles of luggage, or possibly an infant, crying because aroused at that early hour, it was a slow and difficult process. Should the owners of that particular line of steamers enter a caveat for letters-patent on the art of how not to oblige the public, their claim would be speedily recognized by their afflicted and patient patrons.

Our guide-book briefly describes the great city as follows:

"Paris, containing two and a quarter millions of inhabitants, is the most cosmopolitan city in the world. Out of one hundred residents, only thirty are born in the city, and of the remainder (who are principally Belgians and Germans) the English and

Americans number fifteen per cent. Paris covers a surface of twenty-eight and a half square miles, divided into twenty wards, with a mayor to each. But the authority and position usually given to mayors in America are vested in the Prefect of the Seine, who represents the government. Architecturally, **Paris is** a most attractive city, beautified by several large parks and **forty squares,** charmingly arranged and ornamented. Fashion in dress is dictated from Paris, which is also one of the most important of the world's industrial centers, having four hundred and fifty thousand skilled workpeople, and more than one hundred thousand manufacturers."

Of course, the absorbing theme at Paris was the Exposition. Tickets are hawked around the streets by boys, men, and women like so many matches or peanuts. Twenty times within a block they are thrust in your face; not unfrequently crowds of venders, chattering like so many Brazilian monkeys, surround you at once, in their frantic and bewildering zeal to secure customers.

Vast and grand as the Exposition undeniably is, it does not impress one as favorably as our own at Philadelphia in 1876. Much regret especially is expressed that the exhibit from the United States is not more extensive. Aside from the credit of the nation which is at stake, it may serve to deter many Europeans from attending our mammoth show, now finally booked for Chicago in 1893. The Edison electric display was noticeably grand, and the goods of Meriden manufacturers attracted deserved and general attention.

Mr. William E. Gladstone and wife visited the grounds while we were in Paris, and a large crowd soon gathered around them. The "old man eloquent" is still vigorous, considering the fact that he is an octogenarian. Much difficulty was experienced by the police in dispersing the throng of visitors gathered around them. Many purchases were made by both Mr. and Mrs. Gladstone.

Representations of life in Egypt and Greenland by fac-simile street scenes were highly interesting. The Eiffel Tower, costing nearly one million of dollars, is, of course, the chief center of attraction. From morning until late at night the elevator is run at its utmost capacity. Hundreds are constantly awaiting their turn. From three to four hours are consumed in getting people to the top of the structure. Since the cost for the service is five francs, or about one dollar, there must be "millions in it." If Chicago has a tower in 1893 some live and 'cute Yankee will be found who can build an elevator capable of taking two or three hundred up at once if needful.

Another defect of the Exposition is that all directions to the public in the matter of signs and printed notices are in French. As it is a "World's Exposition," why not have translations every-where in the vernacular of all? Hotels, street-cars, public carriages, merchants, and public buildings should be required to translate all notices and price-lists into the leading modern languages at least. Much of the significance of Pentecost would have been lost if the people had not been able to "hear every one in his own tongue."

Americans are here in swarms, though hundreds have already returned. You meet them in the streets, trams, *cafés*, and hotels so frequently as scarcely to realize that you are thirty-two hundred miles from your native land.

At night the great tower, with its calcium light, fire balloons, and many hued illuminations, is grand and impressive, particularly on a star-lit evening, when the symmetrical form and beautiful outlines of the superstructure can be barely traced on the sky and horizon. Undoubtedly it will be permanently retained in the interest of science as a signal service or military point of observation.

THE PARIS SEWERS.—After one of the congresses recently held in Paris, a large party interested in hygiene, led by M. Bechmann, Engineer-in-Chief of Paris, visited the large sewers that run from the Place de la Madeleine to the Châtelet. In barges and in a sort of tramway they traveled through underground Paris. The sewers were illuminated by many lamps, and also by electricity. From a report of the investigation we make a brief extract:

"The barges were supplied with cushioned seats, the ladies came in elegant toilets, and, so that they should not soil their dresses, the steps down into the sewers were carpeted. As an engineering feat these palatial sewers, as they have been so justly described, are certainly most remarkable, and well worth a visit. From the Châtelet the members of the congress were conveyed in comfortable brakes to the sewage farm of Gennevillier. At Clichy they stopped to see the pumping-machines, which lift a third of the sewage and send it over the river in an iron pipe to Gennevillier, where it is used to irrigate seven hundred and fifty hectares of market gardens. The remainder will, in course of time, be sent to Archères and to Méry. In the meantime, two thirds of the sewage of Paris still falls into the Seine at Asnières, and the members of the congress were able to witness how it fouls the waters of the river. They then went over the sewage farm, admired the vegetables, ate some of the fruit, and drank the beautiful, clear water derived from the sewage of Paris. It contained, they were assured, a smaller number of microbes than the best spring water supplied to the city of Paris."

Paris has twenty-seven thousand public carriages, of which twenty-five thousand are under the control of a monopoly. Rapidly driven, you escape from them with difficulty, as they swarm from all points of the compass like the locusts of ancient Egypt. For one franc, about twenty cents, you can be carried a mile or more. The masses take the trams or 'buses, which are crowded to overflowing. When all the seats are occupied the sign "Complet," or full, is displayed, when no more can be received. How different is our American custom, where street-cars are packed as full as a sausage.

The tomb of Napoleon on the banks of the Seine, the Bastile Column, Arc de Triomphe, the Louvre, steam-boat sails on the Seine at a cost of two cents, with four-in-hand drives to various points in the city, constituted some of the sight-seeing of our party during our later visit. Versailles was also seen. It is described as follows by an American author:

"Previous to the reign of Louis XIV. Versailles was used as a hunting-station. About the middle of the seventeenth century that monarch became tired of St. Germains, then the residence of the court, and determined to build a palace that should command the admiration of Europe. The works were commenced in 1660. The architect Levan was the designer. Le Notre was employed to lay out the gardens and grounds, and Le Brun to paint the apartments. In order to obtain sufficient room the whole of the surrounding country to an extent of sixty miles in circumference was purchased, hills were leveled or elevated, and valleys excavated or filled up; to perfect the landscape water was brought from an immense distance to supply the reservoirs and fountains. The actual expense of the whole of this stupendous undertaking was over $200,000,000! The whole court removed here in 1681, and it was the residence of the different monarchs up to 1789. There is no doubt that the enormous amount first expended and that required to keep up such a court impoverished the country, and was the principal cause of the first revolution in 1789. Before that time the population of Versailles was over one hundred thousand; now it scarcely numbers thirty thousand. The number of persons, however, who visit the town on Sundays and *fête* days, when the magnificent fountains play, is very large."

The drive to St. Cloud and Versailles was a never-to-be-forgotten occasion. At the first-named point the ruins of the magnificent palace still remain unrestored. Destroyed by the French guns at Fort Valerian to drive out the Germans, who had gained possession in the memorable and disastrous struggle of 1870, as from this point their fire could destroy any public building in Paris, seven miles distant. it stands as a sad monument of those dark days.

A gambler offered to rebuild it at his own expense, provided he could have the use of it for a short term of years, which was declined. Various other plans for its restoration have been proposed, meeting a similar fate. At some distant day the building will rise, if possible, in grander proportions than before, for the French excel in the art of spectacular display.

THE TUILERIES, PARIS.

CHAPTER VII.

BRUSSELS, THE GAY CAPITAL OF BELGIUM. — A VISIT TO THE BATTLE-FIELD OF WATERLOO. — GERMANY AND THE ROMANTIC RHINE. — HOLLAND, ITS PEOPLE, DIKES, AND WINDMILLS.

"I looked on the field where the battle was spread,
  When thousands stood forth in their glancing array;
And the beam from the steel of the valiant was shed,
  Through the dim rolling cloud that o'er-shadowed the fray.
* * * * * *
I looked on the field of contention again,
  When the saber was sheathed and the tempest had passed;
The wild weed and thistle grew rank on the plain,
  And the fern softly sighed in the low wailing blast."
—*Lord Byron.*

THE harvests throughout Europe in 1886, as a rule, were good. Indian-corn is cultivated on a limited scale, if at all. From the car windows, as I rode thousands of miles, wheat, oats, barley, and other crops were maturing or being reaped in enormous quantities, but not a hill of corn was visible during two months of travel. The damp, rainy, or cloudy weather which prevails much of the time in Great Britain, which the United States has since experienced so largely, with the cheapness of American corn, which literally floods the markets, were assigned as reasons for its neglect, by gentlemen of intelligence with whom I conversed. Very little waste land exists. Swamps are drained and converted into fruitful fields. The hill-tops, denuded of primitive forests, are successfully cultivated even to their very summits. Women toil in the fields by the side of men in great numbers, or with bare feet in some localities, and in wooden shoes or "clogs" elsewhere, convey heavy burdens on their heads to market.

The Sabbath in Brussels presented all the obnoxious features exhibited in Paris, combined with an annual fair which was then in progress. Dense masses of human beings surged through the streets during the day and evening—twenty thousand would not be an extravagant estimate. King Leopold II. is deservedly popular with the people. Following in the footsteps of his father, Leopold I., his administration is generally characterized by tact and good judgment. Like many monarchs, he has several palaces, that at Brussels being the principal one. While the language of Belgium is largely French, it differs essentially from that spoken in Paris, as the unhappy and bewildered tourist soon discovers. It is the fashionable language, though Flemish and Walloon are also spoken, with here and there a sprinkling of English.

At the famous lace manufactory of Brussels I witnessed the intricate and delicate process of lace manufacture. Every description of lace produced was exhibited which would have gladdened the heart of the ladies of America, but I was not an expert. Beautiful and expensive the specimens certainly were. One small collar was offered for sale at $7 50. A sample two inches square could be bought for $1. The bridal veil of the Queen of Belgium was manufactured here, I was informed, on which four hundred persons were employed continuously for a period of six months.

The military museum at Brussels was of interest. Well preserved tapestry made in 1513 was shown. The horse ridden by the Prince of Orange at Quatre Bras and Waterloo in 1815, stuffed, was also among the curiosities.

The vast cathedral of Brussels, begun in 1010, is still unfinished. It is an object of much interest, however, and has many choice paintings and pieces of statuary by several of the old masters. Its bell weighs fourteen thousand five hundred pounds, and is musical as well as sonorous.

In Belgium and France the mode of dispatching railway trains is novel and often amusing. When the hour arrives a man at the station lustily rings a good sized dinner bell; the switchman follows and gives a loud blast from a horn, which he carries with him constantly, to show that the switches are all right;

the guard blows a pocket whistle, which is answered by a vicious and shrill snort of the engine whistle, and the train departs.

As the cars in Europe are generally divided into five compartments, with as many doors opening from the sides, the mode of collecting tickets is also peculiar. On some railways the tickets are taken at the gate as one leaves the station, passengers riding fifty miles or more without showing their tickets. Elsewhere the train stops at the last station but one while the tickets are taken at the car doors. In France the collector walks on the narrow step on the outside of the cars, with the train at full speed, grasping a hand-rail or the open window in the door, and performs the work. As all doors open outwardly, he must be sure that they are well fastened, or fatal results will follow. The utter absence from European cars of the toilet-room, so common on all American trains, is noticeable—a species of barbarism in fact. After riding one or two hundred miles the traveler may enter such rooms at the stations, where men or women in uniform exact from two to four cents for the privilege. Cold water is never found on the trains, except the supply carried for the engine. The sufferings of the miserable tourist who has forgotten to bring a private bottle with him, especially in the intense heat of summer, will be fully appreciated. At the railway stations it would need Diogenes with his lantern to discover drinking-water about the premises after a most vigilant search. Two cents a glass is asked for it at the refreshment room, without ice.

At the battle-field of Waterloo sight-seers still gather from various and distant parts of the earth. I found the field covered with waving grain—some having fallen before the reaper's hand—as thousands perished miserably by shot, shell, and bayonet thrust on that significant and eventful day, June 18, 1815.

Disdaining to ascend the vast conical mound, two hundred feet high, by the long flight of stairs, for personal amusement merely I climbed up the green grassy slopes on the opposite side and interviewed the Belgian lion that surmounts the elevation. The view was one of surpassing beauty. Garrulous guides point out the positions occupied as head-quarters by Wellington and Napoleon, the line of battle of each army, the road over which Blücher came, where Napoleon's Old Guard lay concealed in the corn-field during the day, and where prominent officers met their fearful fate.

Under the mighty mound the dead of both armies were buried. Earth sufficient to complete this mountain in miniature was conveyed from remote portions of the country by peasant women, as the locality is merely a slightly undulating plain.

A horde of hungry peddlers and guides infest the spot. Maps, photographs, bouquets, canes, refreshments, and souvenirs are freely and persistently offered. To decline politely to purchase involves a renewal of the importunity. My steps were dogged for an hour or more from the moment the train arrived. At last, dripping with perspiration and driven to despair, I scattered the crowd with a heroic dose of plain English. The storm of opprobrious epithets which were hurled at my head might not have proved sufficient to disperse the combined armies of Wellington and Napoleon, but were quite emphatic.

While endeavoring to decipher the inscription on a monument erected in memory of the dead of an English regiment, I stepped on a small round stone and turned my ankle. To save myself from falling I sprang quickly forward on what seemed turf. It was a fallen tombstone overgrown with grass. As it inclined considerably, I slid the whole length of it, and fell into a ditch with my ankle badly wrenched. Though groaning with pain, my comical condition caused me to smile. I was the only wounded man on the battle-field of Waterloo, not "dying in the last ditch," but suffering in the first one.

The village of Waterloo is a straggling, insignificant place. It has gradually grown toward the bat-

WATERLOO.

tle-field, but entirely on one street. Houses, barns, stables, and hog-pens are generally joined together, while an intolerable odor is widely disseminated.

"From the top of the mound," says Mr. W. Pembroke Fetridge, "is the best position for surveying the field. It marks the spot where the Prince of Orange was wounded and the very center of the conflict, although on both sides of it, at the farm of la Haye Sainte and the château of Hougoumont, some of the most bloody combats took place.

"There exists a great diversity of opinion in regard to the merits of this memorable event, the number of men engaged, and whether the English had or had not gained the day before **the arrival of the Prussians.** The best English and German authorities say that Napoleon's force was 75,000 men, while the Duke of Wellington's was but 54,000, and only 32,000 of these were of the British or German legion; and the Prussian General Müffling says 'the battle could have afforded no favorable result to the enemy, even if the Prussians had never come up.' The Prussians certainly did not do much execution until after seven o'clock, it being nearly five o'clock before the first regiment arrived. One of our own writers on the subject says: 'In regard to the battle of Waterloo, were we to believe the British accounts, the victory would have remained with them, even though no

Prussians had arrived on the field, while the Prussian and French statements unequivocally demonstrate to the contrary. The British maintained their position with the most obstinate courage; no one doubts that; but, in the language of Gneisenau's official bulletin, " Napoleon continually advanced in masses; and with whatever firmness the English troops maintained themselves in their position, it was not possible but that such heroic exertions must have a limit." And even after the arrival of the fourth Prussian corps under Bülow it is more than probable that the field of battle would have remained in possession of the French. As the result was, it would be difficult to account for the glory which the British and Prussians have taken to themselves for effecting with 140,000 men and 380 pieces of cannon the rout of a French army with 70,000 men and 240 guns, did we not know that the latter was commanded by the French emperor, " who, out of thirteen of the greatest pitched battles recorded in history, had lost but one before the battle of Waterloo."

" Near the building of the farm of la Haye Sainte, which was riddled with shot, is the spot where the brave English Life-guardsman was buried, after having killed nine Frenchmen with his own hand. Near the mound, on either side of the road, are two monuments erected, one to the Hanoverian officers of the

German legion, the other in memory of Colonel Gordon, erected by his family."

The old tavern occupied during the memorable and murderous engagement still stands, which, with a museum of reputed curiosities from the battle-field, attracts many visitors. But little reliance can be placed upon the articles exhibited, or those for sale, since a regular business of manufacturing souvenirs in England and elsewhere has been conducted for many years.

After a brief visit to the memorial church erected in memory of the officers and private soldiers of Great Britain who fell in the memorable contest, I returned by railway to Brussels, twelve miles distant. Had I known that a daily stage ran between the principal hotels of the city and Waterloo for a nominal sum— about $1—with an English-speaking guide, I should certainly have taken it, and thus avoided about three or four miles' walk at Waterloo, no carriage being obtainable at that place.

In the summer of 1890, four years after my return to America, a chaste and appropriate monument was erected by Great Britain on the battle-field of Waterloo, to commemorate the services of the British dead. It is described as follows by an English periodical, and will henceforth constitute an additional attraction to the tourist:

"After a lapse of seventy-five years the remains of the British officers and men who fell on the field of Waterloo have been reinterred in the cemetery of Evere, under a monument unveiled by the Duke of Cambridge before a vast assemblage. The ceremony was of an impressive character, although somewhat marred by the rain. The monument, which is the work of Comte de Lalaing, a Belgian sculptor, who refused to accept any remuneration, represents on a pedestal a kneeling figure of Britannia, with her head bent down as if mourning for her children, and still watching over them in their death sleep. With her trident she points to the sarcophagus where lie her beloved sons; at her feet is the inscription, 'Mortuorum Patria Memor,' on her left is the shield of the mother-country, and a lion standing in a watchful attitude beside the flowing drapery falling from the figure. Two other lions, one couchant, one half roused, guard the coffin, and around helmets, shakoes, tunics, and accouterments are scattered.

"At the back of the statue, over the entrance to the vault, is a black marble slab, on which are inscribed in letters of gold these words: 'In memory of the British officers, non-commissioned officers, and men who fell during the Waterloo campaign of 1815, and whose remains were transferred to this cemetery in 1889, this monument is erected by Her Britannic

Majesty Queen Victoria, Empress of India, and by their countrymen, on a site generously presented by the city of Brussels.' On the side of the door-way to the mausoleum hang three massive bronze shields or targets. They bear the glorious titles of the regiments which fought at Waterloo—guards, dragoons, hussars, artillery, Highlanders, fusiliers, cavalry, and infantry—fitting tokens to be placed upon this hallowed sanctuary. The vault has a narrow passage up the middle. On the right and left are the names of undying fame, though their record is but a roll-call of the dead."

My itinerary in 1886 included a brief visit to Antwerp and a pleasant steamer excursion on the river Scheldt. Large ocean steamers were at anchor in the harbor. The port is one of commanding importance, since it is the commercial metropolis of Belgium. The city possesses an antique appearance, but presents few points of interest. At the huge and venerable cathedral among other paintings of great merit are those of Rubens, Vandyck, and others. The cathedral is 500 feet long and 250 feet wide. Authorities differ concerning the height of the steeple, the estimates varying from 336 to 466 feet. An extensive and picturesque view is afforded from the summit at a cost of one franc for each person.

Germany and Holland were also visited during

the same summer. On arriving in Germany the Rhine, with its numerous vineyards, deserted castles, and countless legends, received my first attention. Daylight was dying as I reached Cologne after an all-day journey by rail from Antwerp. After securing quarters at a hotel I sallied forth to take my first view of the Rhine. Tourists usually confine their observations to the region situated between Cologne and Mayence; the first usually spelled by the Germans "Köln," and the latter "Mainz." From the strong and elegant bridge over the famous river at Cologne the sight was grand. The stream at this point is broad, while the lights on either shore and the gleaming stars that came out of the deepening twilight one by one lent additional charms to the scene.

My stay in the city was brief. I was anxious to witness the greater attractions of the far-famed river further on from the deck of a Rhine steam-boat. The great cathedral, with its beautiful windows and other works of art, is still incomplete, though labor on it began in 1248. Successive monarchs have aided the work, but much still remains to be done.

Women manage the fruit and flower traffic of this city almost exclusively. At five different points I saw groups of women, no fewer than five hundred in all I judged, with white coverings on their heads and blue-checked dresses, seated on the ground in the open air conducting the business.

Cologne derives its name from a Roman *colony* planted here by Agrippina, daughter of the Emperor Germanicus. The streets are narrow and crooked, but cleaner by far than I anticipated. True, the odor of *eau de Cologne*, still manufactured here in large quantities, was not perceptible; but the prodigious statements of writers from time immemorial regarding its festering filth, if ever true, are not so to-day.

Brief pauses of a day or two each were also made on the river at Coblentz and Mayence. Bridges of boats—pontoons—cross the river at the first-named city. A fountain constructed by Napoleon I. while marching to Russia at the opening of that disastrous campaign, with a motto stating by whom it was built, still exists. When the French army was a fugitive mob eagerly returning to Paris the Russians added some sarcastic lines to the structure. I need not quote them.

The cultivation of the vine is the dominant industry in the Rhine region. Up to the mountain peaks every available inch of ground appeared to be under cultivation. Many of the choice brands of wine so freely advertised in the United States, purporting to come from the Rhine valley, are simply drugs. A competent authority, who is engaged in the mercantile business in that section, assured me that certain wines are never sold at all out of the country. They are consumed exclusively in the families of resident rulers, or other persons of distinction.

Opposite Coblentz a mighty fortress, the Gibraltar of the Rhine, is situated. It can accommodate one hundred thousand men. It cost $5,000,000. At this writing it is seriously proposed in German military circles to dismantle the costly and formidable structure, owing to some complications in the present threatening attitude of other European nations. In the judgment of some military men it may prove a menace to Germany, rather than a defense, in case of foreign invasion.

Bingen on the Rhine, the home of the dying soldier boy, over which we wept in youth, is an attractive spot. It was a larger place than I anticipated, containing a population of about eight thousand. Situated at the mouth of the river Nahe, it presented a fine appearance as the sun slowly sank behind the mountain which protects it on the west.

The Castle of Ehrenfels, situated near Bingen, is famous for the tradition concerning Bishop Hatto, and the rats.

It may assume the aspect of downright ignorance or bigotry, but as a whole the Rhine is surpassed by the noble Hudson River. The latter has loftier and grander mountains, a greater volume of water, and more picturesque views. Divest the Rhine of its castles, legends, and antiquity, and no sane man would venture to institute a comparison.

Among other portions of Germany visited were Frankfort-on-the-Main, Cassel, Münster, Hamburg, and Bremen. The narrow and huddled harbor of Hamburg was a surprise to me. Its vast volume of shipping business is conducted in the closest possible quarters. Rotterdam excels it by far, not only as regards its spacious harbor, but in the general attractions of the city. However, extensive efforts were then in progress to increase its capacity, and many antique and costly warehouses were being removed for the purpose. The *débris* made in that portion of the city rendered all traveling, especially pedestrian trips, a disagreeable and dangerous experiment.

My arrival at Amsterdam was unfortunately timed. A riot over some political matter was in progress. The military had possession of the city. In blissful ignorance of all this, I traveled till nearly midnight through the streets in pursuit of a "gasthaus," or hotel. They were distant from the depot, and the Dutch directions were quite confusing, to say the least. It was past midnight when I retired.

The net-work of tree-fringed canals, for which Holland is famous; the public and private buildings, constructed generally of very small brick—the sidewalks often of the same material; the snowy marble stoops, which the women scrubbed with evident delight, were alike novel and interesting. Cathedrals—" doms "— and parks were examined, and excursions to various points made on the adjacent waters.

Many of the public sign-boards seemed like a mixture of Low Dutch and bad English. Possibly " Josh Billings," traveling through the country, took the hint and amassed a fortune thereby. We have space but for a few specimens only: " Watch plaats der stoombooten," waiting place for the steam-boat; " zeil makerij," sail-makery; " blok en pomp maker," block and pump maker; " brood en beschuit bakkerij," bread and biscuit bakery; " melk, boter, kaas," milk, butter, cheese; " to huur," to hire—house to let; " koffy en tree," coffee and tea; and " lodgement—koffy haus," for lodgings and coffee-house. Ship-building, chiefly of iron vessels, is an important industry on the river Maas, though confined necessarily to craft of light tonnage. Holland has an unceasing contest with old ocean to save itself from inundation, from which it was redeemed. Immense sums are expended annually on the dikes. In some localities the houses are situated from thirty to forty feet below the level of the sea. Gateways are so constructed that, in case of invasion by a formidable foreign foe, one human hand could bury the chief portions of Holland under the waters of the North Sea. Drought is of rare occurrence. The proximity of the ocean and the extensive canal system of the country give extraordinary humidity to the atmosphere.

Vast areas of water-lots are constantly being banked in by narrow dikes, or levees. Powerful steam-pumps are then put in motion, which soon remove the water, and after being filled in the ground becomes farms or valuable city lots.

RHINE SCENERY.

CHAPTER VIII.

ON TO SWITZERLAND.—MUSING ON THE MIGHTY ALPS.—LOVELY LUCERNE.—FLORENCE.—MILAN WITH HER MAJESTIC AND COSTLY CATHEDRAL.—THE ETERNAL CITY.—ROMAN RUINS AND MODERN ASPECTS.—A VISIT TO THE VATICAN.

FROM the motley maelstrom of human beings, native and foreign, huddled together at Paris during the Exposition, we start for Lucerne, Switzerland.

Land of William Tell, Winkelried, John Calvin, John Fletcher, Michael Servetus, Rousseau, Madame de Staël, Huber, Necker, and Dumont, all hail! Welcome, ye mighty Alps, with your snow-clad mountains, gushing cascades, and rushing rivers! Land of liberty and deathless patriotism, of grand and rugged scenery, musical boxes, watches, and peaceful homes!

The pale beams of the full moon shimmered on the placid lake, as we arrived at Lucerne at a late hour on Saturday night. Our ride from Paris during the day had covered three hundred and twenty-five miles. The mountain scenery proved a great delight as we approached the border-line between France and Switzerland. A brief stop was made by our party at Basle *en route*.

After a substantial meal at the Hotel Lucernerhof we found rest. Sunday opened with splendor. Mount Righi with difficulty reared its sublime form above the belt of morning mist that environed it; while the rising sun made the beautiful lake, with its romantic shores, numerous boats, and a profusion of fluttering flags, appear like a vast panorama before us.

A popular watering-place, Lucerne abounds with hotels, but has few attractions beyond those furnished by nature. The chiming of church bells was soothing, and the mighty organ at the cathedral a source of inspiration. Time could not be spared for the ascent of Righi or sails on lovely Lake Lucerne, without violating our views and vows regarding the Sabbath. This beautiful sheet of water is full twenty-five miles in length. Clouds around the summit of Mount Righi often shut out the glorious view even after the ascent has been made by wearisome toil.

The merchants depend largely on the patronage of tourists. Carved wood in various forms, views of native scenery, rare stones, canes, clocks, and musical boxes are among the attractions offered the traveler.

The lion monument, by Thorwaldsen, in bass-relief, cut into native rock, is well worth a visit. It was erected in 1821 to commemorate the valor of the brave Swiss Guards who lost their lives in the defense of the Tuileries, August 10, 1792. A dying lion pierced by an arrow is shown. In his expiring moments he places his paw upon a shield, a token of the deathless fidelity of the heroic Swiss who fell in the famous fight.

Many visitors find their way also to the glacier garden. Remarkable bowlders, conveyed to the spot from remote regions by the melting and moving ice of an early period, are displayed in an excellent state of preservation. Most of them are in the form of oval mill-stones resting in deep cavities of the rocks, produced by the law of attrition, from the swirling bowlders amid the waters. Evidences exist that nearly all of Switzerland and much of the northern hemisphere were once covered by immense masses of ice during what is known to geologists as the glacial period. The region at the base of the Alps was then the bottom of the sea, as remains of marine shells and animals abundantly attest.

The permanent population of Lucerne exceeds twenty thousand persons, which reaches greater proportions during the fashionable season, when large numbers of visitors are present. The dominant faith is Roman Catholic. Agriculture and stock-raising receive considerable attention. The scenery is of marvelous beauty. The various mountain peaks surrounding the city average about six thousand five hundred feet in height, while Lake Lucerne occupies an altitude of fourteen thousand feet above the level of the sea.

The day dawned delightfully as our train sped swiftly away from Lucerne and its charming environments, where we had spent the Sabbath. On the margin of the dreamy lake our pathway lies. Small sail and rowboats are awaiting the patronage of the omnipresent tourist, while the handsome steamers give indications of life by faint circles of smoke which arise from their huge funnels, and the decks are being vigorously scrubbed preparatory to their daily trip over the placid waters.

Mount Righi lifts its lofty brow above the surrounding scene, and, as if aware of its own sublime attractions, conceals its crest in a snow cloud. Soon tunnel after tunnel in the mighty Alps is entered— seventy of them during the day. What an expensive roadway! How terribly steep the gradients are! Two engines are required much of the distance to draw the heavily loaded cars. With slow but sure progress the feat is accomplished after an immense amount of puffing and snorting, winding around the mountains on a corkscrew track.

And now we are in the very heart of the wonderful Alps, with their profusion of rugged mountain scenery. Each view, as we slowly glide along, gives grander exhibitions of nature's handiwork than be-

THE MATTERHORN.

fore, if that were possible. On every hand, in the wildest disorder.

"Look, look"—"quick, quick," exclaim many voices simultaneously to their companions as the wonderful panorama passes before them. Now some snow-capped mountain taller by far than its sturdy neighbor catches the eye. A gushing cascade or a miniature cataract like a thread of molten silver falls from mountain peak to the valley below, while yawning chasms, deep ravines, and desolate gorges enhance the sublimity of the picture.

Scattered along the sides of the mountains, or on the edge of dizzy precipices, remote from the busy life of commercial centers, are scattered the humble cottages of the herdsmen and other toilers in these lonely retreats. It is home, and they are content with their plain fare and humble condition, though situated amid these rugged and primeval solitudes. Their love of home and liberty is proverbial.

Arth-Goldau is passed, where sixty years ago an entire village was buried by a landslide. So great was the fall of earth and rock, constituting another mountain almost, that the village was left in its premature sepulcher, while a new settlement grew around and over its site. Here, with the dead buried beneath their feet, many of the inhabitants live, either ignorant of or indifferent to the fate of their unhappy fathers.

Finally the Italian frontier is reached, and the inevitable custom-house examination is renewed. As elsewhere, the chief scrutiny is directed toward the discovery of concealed packages of cigars and brandy. As our party is composed largely of ministers, temperance laymen, and ladies, the search, as hitherto, proves fruitless. No passports have thus far been required, and none probably will be prior to our entering the Turkish Empire.

In Italy, as well as in France, it was harvest time. Women toiling in the hot and dusty fields far outnumbered the men. On every hand were indications of the severe drought, or customary dry season, that had prevailed throughout the region. While New England in common with many Eastern States contended with floods, the reverse had been experienced here. The fields were ashen wastes, except where irrigation had been resorted to. Brooks were dried up— usually raging torrents when the spring opens and the snow melts from the mountains. Even the Arno and the turbid Tiber had dwindled to the insignificance of narrow meadow brooks, which in their reduced fortunes seemed like the veritable sea-serpent finding its way back to the ocean.

After leaving the Alps we pass swiftly over far-reaching plains hundreds of miles in extent. Fertile farms, with a profusion of fruit-trees, including the fig, plum, apricot, pear, and other varieties, are visible by the million. Much of the fruit finds its way to the United States dried and preserved. For the first time I ate figs, ripe and juicy, fresh from the tree. Pleasantly sweet, though inclined to insipidity, they proved to be. The preserved fig as usually sold in our own country will suit the average American better.

Willow used in the manufacture of baskets is largely cultivated. The seed is scattered broadcast, like corn sown for fodder, which gives a harvest of twigs, growing to the dimensions of rye or wheat produced in America. Corn, which does not ripen in England, Scotland, and Ireland, does well in France and Italy. It is cut like hay and spread on the ground to dry. Later the ears are husked in the field and tied in bunches on the sides of barns and hay-stacks to harden in the sun.

Milan, Florence, and other points in sunny Italy are visited. Cathedrals, fortifications, public parks, fashionable thoroughfares, where the rich live in luxury, and narrow, dirty lanes, with a superabundance of festering filth, and where the poor die in doleful garrets, are critically scrutinized.

At Florence I became interested in a poor little hunch-back boy, who, dwarfed by his infirmity, was making his way with difficulty on his crutch through the gaping crowd that surrounded our party. He, among many, was trying to sell guide-books, but could not well be seen owing to the crowd of other venders and sturdy beggars in the way. Having previously bought a book of another dealer, I gave him a small coin as a compromise. With Chesterfieldian politeness he touched his cap to me in acknowledgment, bowing profoundly, meanwhile balancing himself on his crutch. Subsequently, at the cathedral, I sold my guide-book to a member of our party to have an excuse for buying another of the boy. He was evidently overjoyed at his good fortune, and tipped his hat to me gracefully, later, whenever he caught my eye.

Returning to the cathredral, I was chagrined to find that my party had gone by the way of a side door instead of the main entrance, as I expected. After looking in all directions the search was abandoned. My little crippled friend came hobbling up on his crutch and sought to point out the way they had gone, as he could not speak a single word of English. Though I did not overtake them until we met at our hotel at night, I found that a trifling act of kindness on my part had evoked a grateful response from the heart of the unfortunate boy, despite his bent form and ragged raiment.

Mass was in progress at the great cathedral, and we

had an opportunity to hear the grand organ, with a chorus choir of marked sweetness and compass, while the fragrance of burning incense filled the air. The structure, while surpassingly beautiful and imposing without, is comparatively devoid of adornment within.

The great cathedral at Milan is too well known to require a description now. Both the interior and exterior are profusely decorated, while its huge proportions give distinct impressions of awe and sublimity. From the summit a far-reaching view is afforded, which many of our party enjoyed. The roof is absolutely wonderful. There are ninety-eight turrets of the Gothic style of architecture.

Here is a ghastly statue of St. Bartholomew, with his skin off and laid on his shoulder, by some whim of the sculptor. It seemed entirely out of place, and should be consigned to some anatomical museum. Its effect upon some hysterical persons might be productive of a severe mental shock.

St. Ambrose is said to have been buried here. We entered his gloomy cell and sat in his stone chair. San Carlo Borromeo, whose ashes are contained in a case of solid silver so heavy that it must be opened by machinery worked by hand, undoubtedly deserves all the respect for centuries attached to his memory. He was heroic and self-denying during the plague of 1576. He spent a large private fortune to relieve the sick and poor, and went about barefoot, carrying a crucifix, to assist and comfort suffering humanity.

But Italy has produced too many heroic characters for me to linger long at any particular spot—Christopher Columbus, Garibaldi, Michael Angelo, Cavour, and many more. Our party moves on, and we must accompany them.

Rome at last! The city is absolutely disenchanting. Like all European and Asiatic metropolitan centers, it is built of stone and stucco, presenting a somber and funereal aspect. Narrow streets, excepting two or three; comparatively few parks or public promenades, excepting the Pincio region and a few more; destitute of trees or shrubbery of any amount; its dingy high fence walls, especially along the Appian Way, with few sidewalks, furnish a justification for the statement.

Rome has, however, history and antiquity. Here once flourished Julius Cæsar, Nero, and a long line of Roman emperors when Rome ruled the world. Here Paul came to make his "appeal to Cæsar." The chisel of the sculptor, the brush of the artist, the lines of the poet, and the faithful pen of the historian have in some faint degree at least furnished us with important facts.

We have before us both an old and modern Rome. Blocks of new buildings are going up in many quarters of the city, of a showy but shoddy character, however, some of which fall before being occupied. Public improvements are also in progress. Rows of venerable buildings on the banks of the classic Tiber are being torn down to make room for a fashionable

ROME.

promenade along the margin of the river, sheltered by rows of trees like those bordering the Seine in Paris. No doubt it will be a fine improvement when completed, though the pedestrian now gropes his way through narrow streets amid showers of crumbling plaster, stone, brick, and other *débris*.

Rome need not here be described. Suffice it to say that its chief antiquities and objects of interest were seen, including the Vatican, the private chapel of the pope, the Sistine Chapel, with the wonderful and numerous galleries of sculpture, fresco, and painting with which the far-famed " Eternal City " abounds. We also saw the carriages of the pope, which are unexcelled in grandeur by those of any monarch on earth of ancient or modern times.

The columns, arches, ancient walls, gates to the city, baths of Caracalla, the forums, coliseum, catacombs, and other unspecified wonders of the spot were carefully if not critically examined. Carriage-drives along the Appian Way and throughout the principal portions of the city, with strolls at nightfall along the prominent streets of the metropolis, gave favorable conditions for studying Rome as it was and as it is.

Our guide from London to Palestine and Egypt and back to London is Mr. Robert H. Crunden, a profound linguist and a most accomplished scholar. He speaks fluently twelve languages. Alternately he is a shrugging Frenchman, a voluble and gesticulating Italian, or a stolid and emphatic German. His attitude in other lands was equally good. His knowledge of classical and biblical antiquities and localities is simply amazing. Though many scholarly men are members of our party, all by common consent regard him as an authority in these matters.

St. Peter's Church, though often described, must be seen to be appreciated. It is by far the largest and most beautiful church on earth. All that art and mind could do was done to make it the one monumental structure for worship on the face of the globe. The choicest of stones, the mightiest of columns, lofty ceilings, length and breadth of the edifice, statuary, pictures, and adornments of every kind exist. We say pictures to avoid confounding them with paintings—nothing is done in oil. The largest and loveliest pictures are mosaics—eleven thousand stones of different hues being used in one of them. On the ceiling, among many portraits, is one of St. Mark, with pen in hand. From the marble floor it seems like a pen of ordinary size, and yet it is six feet long. The vast building cost $60,000,000, and $500 a week are expended for repairs and cleaning. Rome has three hundred and seventy churches, of which eighty-seven are under the supervision of the representatives of the pope.

Our visit to the Catacombs assumed a weird and sepulchral aspect indeed. We were led by an aged Franciscan monk, who, clad in the humble attire of his order, lighted our pathway down the stone stairway to the abode of the ancient dead, bearing a burn-

CHURCH AT THE CATACOMBS.

ing taper in his hand. Each one of our party also carried a dim light of the same character. Tall and short men, young and old, with two ladies, the entire company clothed in various styles of dress, we doubtless presented a peculiar if not grotesque appearance.

The Italian sunrise and sunset surpass by far those of other lands. Poets and artists have from time immemorial sought to convey some idea of their loveliness. A personal view will alone enable the tourist to fully appreciate their delicate beauty.

No bodies now remain in the Catacombs. The last one was removed many years ago, and the sacred and ancient dust piously buried elsewhere with appropriate religious ceremonies. Many of the most valuable inscriptions carved in marble or other stones have been taken to museums and different places for safe-keeping and the instruction of the student in archæology. The corridors of the Catacombs are three hundred miles in extent.

Some of the designs afford much light on the views of the early Christians regarding the resurrection of the dead. Over the niche containing their remains have been found, rudely carved, the crowing cock, denoting the approach of the morning of resurrection; the fabled Phœnix rising from its ashes; the fish casting Jonah upon the land; and many more suggestive of the same belief. Over the Pagan dead, however, the designs conveyed no sentiment of hope. A racer losing a race, a shattered ship lying upon the rocks, or a broken column, without a single hint of hope, appear in strange and vivid contrast.

At the cemetery of the Capuchin fathers a house filled with human bones is thrown open to the visitor. They are the remains of monks of that order who have died during the past eighteen centuries! The bones are fastened to the ceiling and side walls in various quaint designs in some instances. Most of them are classified and placed in piles like so many articles of merchandise. Skulls by themselves, the bones of the hands and feet in proper order by themselves, besides scapula, clavicle, femur, and other bones of the human body known to anatomy arranged in appropriate heaps with the utmost care. Mummies of monks, dried, withered, with ghastly eye-sockets and grinning teeth, clad in the garments formerly worn by them in life, are also found, crucifix in hand. On the ground floor near them are heaps of fine dust of which their bodies were once composed. Altogether it was a never-to-be-forgotten sight.

Wandering amid the ruins of the Coliseum, the palace of the Cæsars, baths of Caraccala, the Roman Forum, and other important points in this city of antiquities, a peculiar sadness steals over the mind of the thoughtful tourist. Here guests were entertained in the gorgeous palace, yonder was the secret corridor of the monarchs who feared assassination amid the glitter and tinsel of imperial display; there were the baths where sixteen hundred could bathe at once, or elsewhere, the spot where gladiators fought each other or with wild beasts to amuse the eighty-four thousand seated spectators, with twenty thousand more standing within the same structure.

Here are grooves made in the palace pavements by the chariot-wheels of the haughty and wealthy patricians as they gathered from time to time; a pagan altar, where sacrifices were offered over two thousand years ago, with shallow trenches cut in the stone border to hold the blood of the dying animal. Traces of the finest frescoes, costliest mosaics and polished marbles, granite, porphyry, and other stones are visible. Huge columns which could not be moved, even by modern appliances, except with great difficulty, also exist.

Now its glories have vanished. Nero and many nameless tyrants slumber in unknown graves. The Christian martyr no longer is torn by dogs, hungry lions, or daubed with inflammable substances and set on fire to illuminate the gardens of Nero at nightfall. No fire is experienced save the glowing warmth of salvation in the hearts of humble worshipers who gather in nearly four hundred churches in the Eternal City every Sabbath and worship without molestation.

METHODIST EPISCOPAL CHURCH, ROME.

Sixteen of our party attended the Methodist Episcopal mission and partook of the Lord's Supper at the regular Sunday service, which was celebrated at the close of the sermon. Though the discourse was in Italian, we fortunately made the acquaintance of Miss Haugh, the assistant missionary, who by request described the condition and outlook of the movement at a special meeting conducted by us at our hotel in the evening.

After seeing a few remaining points of interest in Rome we departed for Naples, where our itinerary had booked us for three days, including a special trip to the famous ruins of Pompeii, buried by volcanic action A. D. 79. Here the remaining members of our Oriental party joined us.

CHAPTER IX.

AT THE PALACE OF KING HUMBERT.—VESUVIUS VISITED.—EUROPEAN WARLIKE MOVEMENTS.—POMPEII RESURRECTED!—IMPRESSIONS OF GREECE.

"The needle turns away from the rising sun, from the meridian, from the Occidental, from regions of fragrance and gold and gems, and moves with unerring impulse to the frosts and deserts of the North!"— *Walter Savage Landor.*

PRIOR to our departure from Rome we had the unexpected privilege of visiting the royal palace. King Humbert and family were absent, spending a few weeks at watering-places. We found the apartments in process of renovation, though ample opportunity was afforded us to inspect critically the entire suite of rooms usually occupied by the ruling monarch.

The reception rooms, ball, dining, smoking, and other apartments of the royal family were examined with the utmost care. Tapestry and laces of the finest description, with an abundance of mirrors, paintings, statuary, chairs in gilt and velvet plush, with a rare display of other adornments, were freely shown. Even the private chapel of the absent king, contrary to all custom and in violation of explicit orders to the contrary, the person in charge assured us, was thrown open, owing to the potent power and seductive blandishments of timely "tips," in the form of five-franc pieces, from our experienced guide.

For a single moment, indeed, I, with Yankee audacity, ascended the royal steps and sat upon the throne of Italy. An apprehension of being ruthlessly and ignominiously ejected by soldiers "armed to the teeth" in an adjoining room compelled me to retire from the exalted position before suggesting any of the plans for the amelioration of the moral, social, and religious condition of the people which pressed upon my mind. "Uneasy lies the head that wears the crown," asserts the well worn saw; but a Yankee on the throne of Italy is far from feeling unbroken security, knowing that his tenure of office is bounded by seconds rather than years. Such, at least, was my experience. King Humbert possesses fair but not great abilities, and as a ruler is beloved by his people.

Warlike mutterings, ever and anon, are heard in social, commercial, and political circles, and seen in the public press, not only in Italy, but elsewhere in Europe. When we consider the vast number of soldiers distributed throughout the several nationalities of the "old world," who at any moment may be hurled against each other in death grapple at the dictum of a single hot-headed monarch, one may well shudder.

Germany has one million fighting men; Austria

has eight hundred thousand, which number is susceptible of vast increase; while France could in a few weeks place in the field two million additional soldiers. Russia has at her disposal fourteen hundred thousand men, and in an emergency could arm and equip a million more. England is good for a million and a half at the proper moment, while Italy has made noteworthy progress in military matters during the past quarter of a century, and could place an army of six hundred thousand men in motion, unsurpassed in skill and bravery by those of any other nation, in a few weeks, should occasion require. Just now there is an ominous lull. It may or may not precede the inevitable storm of shot and shell that sooner or later will decimate the now happy homes of thousands of families. America, at least, will unite in the hope that the reign of the Prince of Peace may speedily prove world-wide and universal.

Much of the ride to the ancient city of Naples was through orchards of fig, plum, apple, pear, olive, and other fruit-bearing trees. Vegetables apparently receive little attention, unless cultivated near a large and needy market—the great cities. The tall, tapering Lombard poplars, as on the sunny plains of France, are grown in great profusion. How gracefully do their beautiful forms point the hardy sons of labor, who tirelessly toil in these fields year after year, to another and better world, where man rests from his work! Three crops annually are grown in southern Europe. Where fertilization sufficient to meet these immense drafts on the soil comes from is a problem. Comparatively little stock is kept on their farms. Herds of goats, rambling on inaccessible cliffs, flocks of wandering turkeys, the domestic hen, a few donkeys, with here and there a cow, comprise the usual varieties. One large source of supply is the refuse of the cities. Not only the litter from the stables, but the street sweepings, are carefully utilized as well.

The donkey is almost omnipresent. Drawing heavily loaded little carts, or with huge bales, bundles, panniers, or other weights fastened to their backs, surmounted in many instances by a heavy driver, the patient creatures have a hard life of it. Donkey races on the sea-shore constitute some of the varieties of amusements in vogue at certain fashionable watering-places.

Perhaps the most dismal sound emitted from the throat of a domestic animal is the braying of the jackass. Its unearthly and heart-rending noise is heard by day and night, almost continuously, in Eastern countries. It seems to be a cross between the screech of a locomotive whistle, the howl of a wolf, the roar of a lion, or the wail of a lost spirit in Dante's *In-*

ferno. Gazing upon the brute during the operation the scene is grotesque in the extreme. One thinks that the experiment would almost be sufficient to dislocate the neck of the miserable quadruped.

Speaking of this animal recalls an incident related by a Methodist bishop. At a select party several indifferent songs had been sung. Finally the good bishop was asked to sing also. Declining politely, he offered to compromise by relating a story, which was promptly accepted.

"A company of American tourists," he said, "traveling in Egypt, at the close of a hard day's journey, were entertaining themselves by singing several familiar hymns. At the close of one of the pieces a jackass stuck his head through the tent door and brayed vigorously in the most unearthly and distressing manner. As the startled tourists were trying to recover their composure their Arab dragoman entered the tent and in broken English remarked, apologetically: 'You sing a song he tink he know.'" It is needless to remark that the bishop was not asked to make any further contribution to the entertainment of the evening.

As we approach the East it is fully apparent that many of our modern ideas of comfort and civilization are practically ignored. On the arrival of our train at Brindisi we waited nearly an hour for the protracted and wearisome *table d'hôte* dinner to begin, though it had been ordered three days before. Time was precious and our steamer would soon sail. One wash-basin alone was available for twenty-six persons, who waited until other members of the party had completed their ablutions.

At the wharf, in the darkness of the night, we groped our way along with difficulty to reach a rowboat, which was to convey us to the steamer, about to leave for Patras, Greece. Then, with difficulty, and in danger of breaking one's bones in case of falling, we climbed up a rope ladder to the deck. On leaving the steamer at the end of the route the small boat was again brought into requisition to convey us to the shore. The possibility of dredging the channel or of building a pier over the shallow water evidently has not entered the mind of the stupid authorities.

During our tarry at Naples a side trip was made to Vesuvius, which had been in an active state for several months. Though the ascent was accomplished with difficulty, the panoramic view of Naples and its wonderful bay, with Capri, the resting place of brave old Garibaldi, and other adjacent islands, was a great delight. Down into the fiery and awful throat of Vesuvius we gazed. For a few moments the view was clear and unobstructed in any manner. At brief intervals, with terrific snorts and puffing like an immense blast-furnace, masses of lava and other *débris* were shot into the air to the height of perhaps one hundred and fifty feet, which fell in showers in every direction. The spectacle was sublimely grand and not wholly destitute of a spice of personal danger.

For a franc (about twenty cents) our guides would run to the very edge of the belching monster and place a coin or key from your pocket into the molten lava. When cool the pieces are carried home by tourists as souvenirs. All the mountains in the vicinity and for miles distant, even as we approach the Ionian Isles and Grecian Archipelago, give undisputed evidence of their volcanic origin.

Vesuvius is perhaps the oldest active volcano. Many others, once terribly destructive, have become absolutely extinct. Strabo erroneously declared in his day that this was then the condition of Vesuvius. He was totally and terribly mistaken.

The burial of seven towns, A. D. 79, by this volcano, including Herculaneum and Pompeii, can never be effaced from the pages of history; nor can its frightful and destructive violence in our own day, notably in 1822 and 1872. Even now the foremost and most conspicuous scientists of modern times, including Professor Palmieri, regard its present indications with grave apprehension. Examinations by competent experts are regularly made, in order that timely warning may be given to the people in the valley and on the sunny slopes of the fiery monster. The cultivation of the grape in numerous vineyards is being carried well up its sides. Great clusters of the ripe and delicious fruit, together with an abundance of figs, gladdened the eye as we made our progress slowly upward.

Pompeii! Here is the city of silence! Street after street without vehicles or pedestrians save a few visiting tourists; stores without goods or customers; residences of the rich and poor, with no one at home, and temples of lust, with brazen, disgusting, and obscene emblems, happily destitute of occupants or victims. It has been said by a recent writer that all cities have places of similar low character, which is a lamentable fact. But it may be doubted whether similar degrading advertisements of the business were ever displayed elsewhere on the face of the globe.

Comparatively few lives were lost at the time of its burial in volcanic mud and ashes over eighteen centuries ago, timely warning having been given. The sidewalks and heavy stone pavements are well preserved, as are most of the buildings. Grooves made in the streets by the Roman chariots are plainly visible. Fountains, baths, bakeries, the doctor's office, and other places still remain. In some instances painted signs on the stuccoed walls of stores exist, showing the kind of business that was conducted at the spot. Even the ancient cemetery has been exhumed, revealing well-preserved monuments describing the virtues of the departed, one a boy of twelve years of age.

We drank at the old well that quenched the thirst of the inhabitants of Pompeii before its disastrous overthrow. In many places the walls of buildings have been restored in a measure to prevent utter destruction and decay. Soldiers guard the spot, by direction of the Italian authorities, to prevent vandalism on the part of visitors.

Eighty loaves of bread were found in the oven of the public bakery during the earlier excavations, where they had been left by the fleeing proprietor. The elder Pliny lost his life at the time the city was destroyed, and to the younger Pliny we are indebted for much valuable information relative to its fate. Thirteen skeletons were found in one house, of which five were the remains of females. The panic was so great that the rich sought safety at the homes of the plebeian, who in turn fled for refuge to the palace of the patrician. Many bodies were found in extensive wine-vaults. Some who had escaped lost their lives in returning for their valuables, which were found by their remains, and from the skeleton of others belts of gold and silver were subsequently taken. Owing to the fact that the great amphitheater was filled with many of the people attending some sort of a play in the open air outside of the walls of the city, and the timely warning given, to which reference has been made, the loss of life was reduced, comparatively, to a minimum point.

The acoustic properties of the vast amphitheater are remarkable. Repeated experiments made by members of our party proved that every word spoken could be distinctly heard at the remotest portion of the structure, though uttered in a moderate tone of voice. Excavations are still in progress, though carried on in a straggling and unsystematic manner, with few laborers. Competent engineers and a full force of men, such as were employed at Johnstown, Pa., after its fatal destruction, would accomplish the entire work in a period of three months. And yet sporadic efforts have been in progress for more than seventeen centuries!

The sail from Brindisi to Patras, already noted, was one of quiet yet solid satisfaction. Islands around which so many classical associations cluster in song, tradition, or sober history lent peculiar charms to the voyage. With a silent sea, cloudless sky, and a balmy atmosphere one seemed almost in a pleasant dream.

Corfu, where we touched for a few hours to receive and discharge passengers and freight, presented an attractive appearance. The buildings, like most of those in southern Europe, were of the yellowish white stone, or stucco, already described.

A fleet of small boats surrounded us with almost magical promptitude on our arrival, to convey passengers to the shore. Like other Eastern harbors, no effort is made to deepen the channel or construct a pier to accommodate vessels of much draught of water.

Cases of wine, empty wine-casks, some iron tubing, with a few other articles, comprised the amount of freight left by our steamer, which served to indicate the limited business done at this far away and obscure locality. Steamers flying various national flags were lying peacefully at anchor in the land-locked harbor, one being an Italian school-ship where young men were being trained for the navy of that country. Corfu, after many changes during its past history, now belongs to Greece.

Patras was reached in the early dawn of the following morning. Amid a crowd of peddlers, beggars, or porters desiring to carry luggage, we found our way to the custom-house. After a superficial examination we were soon on board the Grecian railway train *en route* to Athens.

We pass near Misolonghi, capital of Ætalia. It has sustained stubborn and protracted sieges. Marco Bozzaris, with a force of four hundred patriots, defied a Turkish army of fourteen thousand men, which finally withdrew, for two months. Lord Byron, who contributed £12,000 to the cause of Greece, and organized a brigade at his own expense, died here April 19, 1824. As our train glides onward we reflect upon his extraordinary gifts and poetry, his unhappy domestic life, dissolute character, and his peculiar if not unnatural mother.

As a solemn admonition to smugglers, we learned at Patras that one detected in the act at that port two days before we landed had been fined 1,800 francs, and was then serving a term of imprisonment in the common jail besides. Patras is memorable in Grecian history from the fact that near the spot a complete victory was achieved over the Turks in one of their earlier campaigns. Mount Parnassus lifts its lofty and classical brow with seeming pride as our train glides on to its destination.

At one of the numerous stations we see for the first time wine in skin bottles. Then the biblical allusion concerning putting new wine into old bottles is suggested.

We passed through the celebrated currant region, where annually large quantities of the dried fruit are exported to America and elsewhere. The currants are packed in hogsheads for shipment. As we went by men were standing in the half-filled casks, stamping energetically with their heavy shoes to make room for more of the fruit then being brought to them. The ladies of our party contemplated the spectacle with evident disgust, and declared that henceforth the dried fruit used by them should be washed more carefully than ever.

It was a long ride to Athens. In order to catch the train we went without our breakfast, save a roll and a bunch of luscious grapes procured near the depot. A royal and substantial meal, ordered by telegraph by our thoughtful tourist conductor, awaited us at one P. M. at an intermediate point, however. Small armies have frequently won great victories, at least it was so in this instance, as our hungry party made a vigorous onslaught on the toothsome viands placed before us. Not even a single small "basket of fragments" remained at the close of that meal, much less twelve, as recorded in the biblical narrative of the miracle of the loaves and the fishes.

Modern Athens is an attractive place. Fine marble buildings, broad drives and sidewalks, horse railroads, with all the conveniences of modern times, render it the delight of the average tourist. To be sure, some drawbacks existed. It was the dry season, and the earth and air abounded with a white dust ground by attrition from the stones of the street. Vegetation seemed nearly extinct—no green grassy lawns or fields of verdure, and, like much of southern Europe, no visible forests.

Mutilated coin, so much abominated in the United States, circulates freely throughout the East. The climax had evidently been reached in Athens. Desiring a draft to be cashed, to my deep disgust the entire amount was paid me in punctured gold coin, all the holes being of considerable size. I was very careful to exchange them for other money before sailing for Smyrna. Such debased coin is as eagerly received by merchants and other business men as similar coin was in America a few years ago before the craze for its extermination began.

Continental Greek is the chief language spoken, with a sprinkling of English, German, and French. The university at Athens has fourteen hundred students, nearly all of whom are natives of Greece. A high-school also exists, which has a good reputation.

Professor Van Benschoten, of Wesleyan University, Middletown, Conn., delights to tell the following incident: Entering a *café* at Athens, he called for canned corned beef in his best Greek, being a recognized Greek scholar. Large quantities of the

STATUE OF JUPITER OLYMPUS.

meat are imported from the United States. The waiter said, apologetically, in Continental Greek:

"We have no canned corned beef, but we have some canned"—then pausing a little to show that he knew at least one word in English, he repeated—"but we have some canned language," meaning tongue, the Greek word γλῶσσα (*glossa*) for tongue and language being identical.

Much to the regret of many tourists and all archæologists the Acropolis and other classical ruins in Athens are fast crumbling to decay. Some effort must be made by the government or archæological societies to conserve and restore them for future generations, or it will be too late. Huge blocks of finely chiseled marbles, bearing important Greek inscriptions, lie outside the walls of the Acropolis, hopelessly shattered. How sad are all the surroundings. Where sages, philosophers, scholars, warriors, and statesmen formerly assembled only a few straggling goats could be seen as I went at the dawn of day to view the sunrise. Some Grecian tramps, who had spent the night amid the mighty columns, crawled forth at my approach. *Sic transit gloria mundi.* What thoughts press upon the mind, reflecting as we do that we are in the land of Homer, Socrates, Xenophon, Galen, Alcibiades, and other famous men of by-gone ages.

At five P. M. Sunday a religious service was conducted on Mars' Hill by members of our party. Prof. D. R. Dungan, the Rev. Dr. Porteus, the Rev. Dr. Stone, of Hartford, and the author took part. The retiring American consul was also present, the Hon. Mr. Moffat, of New Jersey. He returned to the United States the following week.

MARS' HILL.

The Rev. Dr. T. De Witt Talmage, who preached on Mars' Hill a few weeks later, said: "Though more classic associations are connected with this city than with any other city under the sun, because here Socrates and Plato and Aristotle and Demosthenes and Pericles and Herodotus and Pythagoras and Xenophon and Praxiteles wrote or chiseled or taught or thundered or sung, yet in my mind all those men and their teachings were eclipsed by Paul and the Gospel he preached in this city and in your near by city of Corinth. Yesterday, standing on the old fortress at Corinth, the Acro-Corinthus, out from the ruins at its base arose in my imagination the old city, just as Paul saw it. I have been told that for splendor the world beholds no such wonder to-day as that ancient Corinth standing on an isthmus washed by two seas, the one sea bringing the commerce of Europe, the other sea bringing the commerce of Asia. From her wharves, in the construction of which whole kingdoms had been absorbed, war-galleys with three banks of oars pushed out and confounded the navy-yards of all the world. Huge-handed machinery, such as modern invention cannot equal, lifted ships from the sea on one side and transported them on trucks across the isthmus and set them down in the sea on the other side. The revenue officers of the city went down through the olive-groves that lined the beach to collect a tariff from all nations. The mirth of all people sported in her Isthmian games, and the beauty of all lands sat in her theaters, walked her porticoes, and threw itself on the altar of her stupendous dissipations. Column and statue and temple bewildered the beholder. There were white marble fountains into which, from apertures at the side, there rushed waters every-where known for health-giving qualities. Around these basins, twisted into wreaths of stone, there were all the beauties of sculpture and **architecture**, while standing as if to guard the **costly display** was a statue of Hercules of burnished Corinthian brass. Vases of terra-cotta adorned the cemeteries of the dead—vases so costly that Julius Cæsar was not satisfied until he had captured them for Rome. Armed officials, the corintharii, paced up and down to see that no statue was defaced, no pedestal overthrown, no bass-relief touched. From the edge of the city the hill held its magnificent burdens of columns and towers and temples (one thousand slaves waiting at one shrine), and a citadel so thoroughly impregnable that Gibraltar is a heap of sand compared with it. Amid all that strength and magnificence Corinth stood and defied the world."

CHAPTER X.

DEPARTURE FOR SMYRNA.—THE LAND OF PASSPORTS.—A FEVER-SMITTEN CITY.—MOUNT PAGOS.—THE GRECIAN ARCHIPELAGO.—AN EXCURSION TO EPHESUS.—AT THE BIRTHPLACE OF SAUL.

WE left Athens with its wealth of classical associations and never-to-be-forgotten ruins with emotions of deep regret. Weeks and months indeed might be spent in the ancient and time-honored city and environs with increasing interest and profit. But the hour of departing is inexorable. Other and more distant lands remain to be visited. Turkey, Palestine, and Egypt, including numberless places clothed with historical, biblical, or legendary suggestions, lure us onward.

A final and delightful carriage-drive conveyed our party through the most prominent streets of Athens to Piræus, its sea-port. It is distant five miles, with a good road, though the hot and dusty season is oppressive. Daily communications are also made by railway trains.

Piræus is situated on a peninsula and boasts of three harbors, one being set apart for ships of war. Until the termination of the protracted Persian War

Phaleron was the recognized port of Athens. Themistocles, seeing the vast strategic importance of a change, inaugurated the movement. Later generations have fully appreciated his sagacity. Piræus finally fell before the fury of Sylla and his indomitable warriors, and subsequently dwindled into comparative insignificance. During the days of Strabo it had degenerated into a straggling village, presenting few indications of its former importance. The growth of the modern town can be traced no further than the year 1834. Its harbor, though naturally good, like all Eastern sea-ports is allowed to fill up gradually with sediment until even ships of moderate draught are compelled to anchor some distance from the shore.

For the first time on our journey we now require passports, since we sail to Smyrna, where flies the Turkish flag. Armed with a polite note of introduction from Mr. Walker Fearn, then our popular United States minister at Athens, three of us were driven rapidly to the residence of the Turkish consul-general at Piræus. Our steamer would sail in two hours, hence there was no time to be lost.

Unfortunately, we arrived a few minutes before office hours. Vigorous and repeated knocks finally aroused a sleepy clerk. He took the letter from the American minister with a lofty manner of disdain, and disappeared to receive orders from his superior, the vice-consul, who was lost in the mazes of an afternoon Turkish siesta. At length he returned, with a shrug and an atmosphere of contempt at the Christian dogs who did not happen to know his office hours. He was evidently a novice at the work, and was soon obliged to call his superior, who finally appeared. With evident ill-humor and insufferable *hauteur* he completed the business. By his own blunder he had placed the name of a lady and gentleman of our party, practically strangers to each other, on one passport, much to their annoyance. While the mistake was being explained to him he shrugged his shoulders, elevated his nose, and disappeared, leaving the party to make the best of it, while he jingled his fees—many five-franc pieces—in his pocket.

The steamer's route from Piræus to Smyrna was of a serpentine character. Through the sleeping waters of the Ægean Sea, or Grecian Archipelago, which separates Greece from Asia Minor, we pursued our course. The days were clear and the atmosphere balmy. Islands, near and remote, reared their blue outlines from the surrounding sea with a delicious and dreamy appearance. All were of a mountainous character, with unmistakable evidence of their volcanic origin. What important events of song and story are associated with these quiet waters and graceful, tapering, mountain peaks! Contending armies have met,

The wail of the dying has mingled with the triumphant shout of victory. The prince and the peasant—lovers, warriors, and even nations, that once flourished amid these suggestive surroundings, have vanished like very vapors.

Chios, or Scio, its modern name, is reached. It is the first land under Turkish rule yet sighted. Conquered in the fourteenth century, the inhabitants were barbarously butchered by their captors, the bloodthirsty Turks. Later, it fell into the hands of the Genoese; but was subsequently re-captured by the same power, which has mercilessly ruled it ever since, though insurrections have been of frequent origin. Ion the tragedian, Theopompus the historian, and Theocritus the sophist were born here.

Owing to the shallow water the steamer anchored fully one half of a mile from the shore. In a few moments the ship was surrounded by a fleet of small boats, seeking to convey passengers and baggage to the shore. The din was doleful and the tumult indescribable as the half-clad, sturdy, and swarthy natives vociferated wildly. Finding but two or three passengers to take to the land, many climbed upon the deck of the steamer with articles for sale. Strange confections, or jellies, in glass tumblers, were offered, but found no purchasers, doubt being expressed regarding their composition and utility. I compromised and purchased some peanuts from an innocent-looking vender, but soon regretted my choice, since their antiquated flavor failed to evoke the respect ordinarily due to extreme old age. Had they been preserved since the close of Mahomet's career, they could scarcely have been less palatable.

The government salt-works are situated here. On the sea-shore, long before we anchored, huge conical heaps of salt, like tents in appearance, attracted our attention. There were more than one hundred and fifty of them by actual count. The commerce of the place is extremely limited, however, since the island has not yet recovered from the disastrous and terrible earthquake of 1881, when four thousand lives were lost. Silk, wool, and cotton, with a variety of tropical fruits, constitute its chief productions.

Throughout all Oriental countries isolated and straggling buildings are seldom seen. Unlike the United States, cities and villages are usually built compactly together of stone. The origin of the style can be satisfactorily traced to the primitive period, when consolidation was absolutely essential in order to secure protection from enemies in war and roving bands of robbers at all times.

Smyrna proved to be smitten with a species of malarial fever, brought from India, known as the "dangee." No fewer than fifty thousand cases had

COLOSSUS OF RHODES.

occurred, though the deadly scourge was abating materially at the time of our arrival. Evidently it was not a desirable place for a prolonged visit. In fact, when our two days allotted for inspecting the quaint and ancient city had expired we took the French steamer for Beirut with keen satisfaction, the unanimous opinion being expressed that it was a good place to sail away from. During our rambles about the place we saw camels outside of a menagerie for the first time in our experience. The streets, dark, narrow, and crowded, were full of them. Usually fastened together in droves of five or six, they were laden with grapes, figs, and other native products brought from various parts of Asia Minor on their way to the United States and other distant markets. The ungainly forms of the camels, with the tinkling of bells fastened to their necks, the quaint architecture of the buildings, together with the flowing garments of the drivers and people, served to furnish an Oriental picture at once unique and interesting to the wanderers from the West.

Dogs by uncounted dozens, slumbering on the narrow sidewalks in the heat of the day, compelling us to alter our course lest we should step on them, snapped at us as we passed, or darted into a neighboring alley with a low and defiant growl. The population of the city is estimated at two hundred thousand, which is divided among the Turks, Greeks, Jews, Armenians, and Franks. All tourists love to frequent the bazaars. Though many articles of a curious or ornamental character are offered for sale, the shops are as a rule dingy, dirty, and labyrinthine. Business is transacted largely by English, French, Italian, and Dutch merchants.

Smyrna, with six other localities, claims that the immortal Homer was born on her soil.

> "Seven cities claim old Homer, dead,
> Through which the living Homer begged his bread."

Here was one of the original seven churches of Asia, described by the apostle John in the Book of Revelation. Its origin has been satisfactorily traced to Alexander the Great. Among its exports are cotton, dried fruits, silk, camel's and goat's hair, wool, and opium, while its imports include coffee, sugar, indigo, alcoholic liquors, iron, steel, lead, and tin.

The Rev. Dr. D. S. Schaff, who made a similar tour a few months previous to the arrival of our party, recorded his impressions in that most excellent paper, the New York *Mail and Express*, from which we make extracts. He says concerning Smyrna:

"One of the odd sights on the streets of Smyrna is the turkeys. The Smyrnese drive them in flocks as we do sheep, and keep them in order with long rods.

"The articles of export are dried fruits, olive-oil, grains, and rugs; these fill extensive warehouses. Smyrna is the principal source of supply, after Spain, of licorice root. The acorn of the valorea oak is brought to the city in large quantities, and the hull, which secretes tannin, is shipped to England, Russia, and especially Trieste for tanning purposes. The annual export of raisins amounts to twenty thousand tons, and they are worth from twenty-seven to forty-seven shillings a hundred-weight on the vessel. The grapes are picked when ripe, and dipped in potassium and water to facilitate the processes of drying and preservation. While the Smyrna merchants ship no grade of raisins equal in quality to the raisins of Malaga, they deal in small sultanas exclusively. They are seedless, light, golden in color, and translucent, and grow only here and in small quantities at Damascus.

"The fig-market of Smyrna is the largest in the world. Like the raisins, they pass through commission merchants to the packing-houses. I visited the warehouse of Mr. Krikorian, an intelligent Armenian who speaks English and whose brands are well known abroad. The fig is allowed to fall from the tree and is allowed to remain on the ground for three or four days till it is thoroughly dried. They are then gathered into goat's-hair bags, holding three hundred and twenty pounds, and carried to the city by team or camel. In the warehouses they are thrown in heaps upon the stone floor and assorted by women into different grades. The women keep their hands moistened with salt water, which gives the fruit a gloss, makes it pliable, and helps to preserve it. The poorer qualities are packed in bags, the poorest being sent principally to Marseilles, where they are used for vinegar and spirits. The better qualities are carried to tables, and pressed by men into shape and packed for the market. The flat or pressed figs, called also pulled figs, are preferred by the American consumer. The lacoums, or figs more loosely packed, are preferred by the English. The best qualities are packed in boxes. Mr. Krikorian manufactures his own boxes. The packing season lasts from August 10 to November 1. The annual shipment from Smyrna is five thousand tons, varying in price from twenty-three to thirty-four shillings a hundred-weight, delivered on board ship. The best figs are grown in the district between Ephesus and Adin. The fruit grown on the islands does not keep, and is not adapted for export. The fig-tree does not bear until it is twelve years old, unless the ground is carefully cultivated. The establishment of Mr. Krikorian alone employs two hundred and seventy men and women. . . .

"Smyrna was one of the earliest stations occupied

by the American Board. Pliny Fisk and Levi Parsons, the first missionaries, began to labor here in 1820. The visible results have not been as satisfactory at this sea-port as in the inland cities, but the place is a strategic point and must be held. I missed the Rev. Lyman Bartlett and Mr. McNaughton, who were off in the interior on a preaching tour, as also the Rev. Mr. Constantine, a converted Greek, but found the ladies and school-teachers at home, and had the pleasure of visiting the girls' school, which is attended by fifty day and fifteen boarding scholars. The mission also conducts a school for boys and a kindergarten. The buildings are ample and commodious. No one at a distance can form any adequate idea of the pleasant and restful contrast between the aspect of the mission premises in these Eastern cities and their surroundings. Going into them and breathing their atmosphere, freighted with the culture of Christian society, is like drinking from a fresh and living fountain by the dusty way. The Baptists have a mission, and the Scotch work among the Jews."

The ascent of Mount Pagus, on foot, during a day of torrid heat, will not soon be forgotten. A few of our party rode up the mountain on donkeys, followed by donkey boys who urged the unhappy brutes to their utmost speed, which seldom exceeded a walk. At length the summit was reached, and a panoramic view of entrancing beauty rewarded us. The vast city with mosques and minarets was spread before us, bordered by the broad and beautiful bay.

Near the top of the mountain the grave of Polycarp is shown. He was the first Bishop of Smyrna. Here the first Christian church in Smyrna is said to have stood. The place is still carefully pointed out to tourists as one of the antiquities of the city. A rude mosque now occupies the site of the ancient structure. Rags attached to sticks near the spot fluttered in the gentle breeze. They were torn from the clothing of invalids by friends and brought to the sacred site, under the impression that health would thereby return once more. Our conductor cautioned us against approaching a certain spot where a rude mat was placed with some attempt at decoration, since it was regarded as a holy situation. Death has been inflicted on some presumptuous but thoughtless visitor who went too far in his curiosity.

Smyrna has very bad drinking-water, and the strictest temperance man is puzzled to know what to drink in that fever-smitten city, especially at meals when tea and coffee are not served. At different periods the cholera and plague have decimated the population, while terrific earthquakes have been experienced, notably in A. D. 178 and 1846. By a destructive fire in 1841 more than twelve thousand buildings were swept away in a few hours, as the appliances for extinguishing conflagrations were and are exceedingly primitive.

An evening visit was made to the "Smyrna Rest," for seamen, on the quay fronting the bay. A big, honest-looking leader was in charge. A few years ago he entered a Bowery Mission, New York, as a drunken sailor. He was converted, and now makes it his life-work to conduct a similar mission for the reformation of sailors touching at Smyrna. A coffee and reading room are connected with the enterprise.

Few books were found, and the supply of papers quite limited, though printed in several languages. None were of recent date.

The prayer-meeting held nightly, for seamen and visitors chiefly, was of interest, though disturbed by the noise from the *café* in the room adjoining. Several of our Palestine party attended service. With limited means the mission is doing good, and deserves financial aid from Christians elsewhere. The Rev. Mr. Constantine is understood to be the official head of the movement. He was present one evening when our company visited the mission.

Before sailing from Smyrna a side trip to Ephesus was made by railway. Here also was one of the seven churches of Asia. It is distant from Smyrna fifty miles. But few traces of its former grandeur remain. A section of the great Roman aqueduct, foundations of the famous temple of Diana, and other prominent structures alone exist.

This renowned temple, so dazzling that visitors were cautioned to look out for their eyesight on entering it, was four hundred and twenty-five feet long and two hundred and twenty feet wide. The roof was of cedar, which was supported by one hundred and twenty-eight columns sixty feet high. The statue of the goddess Diana was composed of ivory, profusely decorated with ornaments of gold. According to a well authenticated tradition this magnificent temple—**justly** styled one of the seven wonders of the world—was entirely consumed by an incendiary fire. A misguided miscreant, Erostratus by name, confessed the crime; his desire being an eternity of disgrace, knowing that in this form his name would descend to remotest posterity.

Horses, bony, sore, spavined, and ring-boned, were in readiness to take the party to distant points of interest. After all were supplied, I mounted a miserable bony brute, the only one remaining, astride of a rough Turkish saddle, where buckles, straps, and needless bunches suggestive of the torture of the Inquisition were plentiful, and which soon removed much cuticle from my lower limbs. All the animals were fresh from the plow, really the best available, since they were to be used but two or three hours. My superannuated quadruped could not be coaxed out of a walk. To confess the naked truth, owing to my inexperience as a horseman and to the buckles and bunches aforesaid scraping the surplus flesh from my body, I was not especially ambitious that he

THEATER AT EPHESUS RESTORED.

should quicken his pace. I rode as far as the cave in which the early Christians conducted their services, it being the first church of Ephesus, which I entered and carefully examined.

Here I surrendered the aged horse to a native attendant, and returned on foot to the hotel, examining various ruins by the way. Whether Paul actually "fought with beasts at Ephesus" or not has for centuries been an unsolved problem in theological circles. Whatever were the facts in his case, personally I retained distinct and painful impressions of my experience with this venerable and cadaverous beast at the site of the same city for many days after my visit. Our party returned later, but in good season for a substantial dinner at the Ephesus hotel.

Ephesus is simply a desolation. The threat to "blot her out," recorded in the Book of Revelation, has been amply fulfilled. She did not repent, and for long centuries no Christian Church has existed there. The cave of the Seven Sleepers, where seven young Christian fugitives are said to have slept two hundred years and found Christianity triumphant on awakening, St. Luke's grave, and many other apochryphal localities are pointed out to the credulous tourist.

In the stone walls around some of the farming land fragments of capitals, friezes, columns, and other portions of the ancient temple and other edifices can be seen. What an ignoble end of a mighty career! Much curiosity exists among archæologists as to the whereabouts of the vast quantities of building material of which these structures were originally composed.

Thousands of acres of unfenced land, covered with myriads of cobble-stones, are seen on every hand.

How the average goat manages to exist during the dry season is an unsolved problem, since vegetation is absolutely invisible, the entire country being, so to speak, a bed of hot ashes, gleaming beneath a brassy and burning sky.

We returned to Smyrna at an early hour, finding rest and food at our superb hotel, which overlooked the waters of the bay.

In rocking, tossing, small boats we bade a long farewell to Smyrna on the following day, and were rowed to the French steamer anchored off shore. Occasional splashes of water swept over us, caused by the strokes of the oars and unskilled rowing of the native boatmen. The ship was reached in safety.

We found the steamer well filled, though ample accommodations had been reserved for our party through the foresight of our conductor. Third and even fourth class passengers are taken on these steamers. The latter bring their own provisions and bedding, and sleep on the deck in the open air. However, in that warm climate, where no rain or dew falls for several months, it involves no hardship worth naming. Turks, with their wives and children huddled into curtained corners of the main deck, indifferent to the presence of representatives of nearly all nations about them, are passengers.

The sea continues "as calm as summer's evenings

ISLE OF PATMOS.

be" in the entire water portion of the journey between Brindisi, Italy, and Beirut, Syria. By this route one is constantly in sight of land—usually some place famous in the annals of history, which lends a peculiar charm to the entire journey, reviving as it does the studies of one's youth.

The Isle of Patmos displayed its shadowy outlines in the gray dawn of the morning, though too far to secure distinct impressions. Since it was not included in our itinerary, no stop was made. It seemed like a gloomy though quiet and sequestered spot. St. John the apostle, banished to this lonely retreat by the emperor Domitian, A. D. 95, wrote here the Book of Revelation, and possibly the Gospel of John, during his confinement. It is a desolate, rocky region, the entire island being but twenty-eight miles in circumference. At the time of his incarceration it was merely a Botany Bay for the imprisonment of criminals and political offenders. Tourists are shown the spot where St. John is said to have received the communications from heaven, but few if any of them venture to believe in it.

Tarsus is but ten miles distant from Messina, but the progress is slow, since the roadway is in poor repair and the two trains each way daily are of a mixed character, combining both freight and passengers in their make-up. British capitalists own the railway, and an English-speaking conductor gave us an opportunity to glean information concerning the country. The passenger cars were fairly comfortable, with divans in portions of them for the special accommodation of the traveling Turk, who cannot enjoy life unless he tucks both feet crosswise beneath him, sitting on his heels tailor fashion.

At various places along the route the cotton crop was being gathered, elsewhere the work had been completed, and naught but barren fields of dry stubble were visible. A Turkish officer entered our car and began to take our names, residence, destination, business, asking a variety of other equally impertinent questions. Our watchful tourist conductor soon called him one side, and slipped a fee into his itching palms, when he abandoned his investigations, seemingly begun in the interest of the government. As the miserable Turkish soldier is half clad, often going in rags waiting for promised uniforms which are seldom seen, without even his small salary being paid him, in sheer desperation he is driven to bribes and petty swindles "to keep soul and body within speaking distance of each other," as an erratic Methodist preacher once put it in describing his unavailing efforts to live on a low salary tardily paid.

Tarsus traces its origin to the period of Sardanapalus. It is certainly of very great antiquity. Many important events have taken place within its borders. Situated on the right bank of the river Cydnus, it is surrounded by an extensive and productive plain of great fertility. As in most Eastern countries, the houses are built of a species of native stone, with flat roofs, presenting a squatty appearance. Rude bazaars crowd close to the streets, with a meager display of primitive wares needed by the native population. Dark and dirty loaves of bread, flat as the proverbial pancake, were being baked before a crackling fire of roots and branches of trees in a bakery, in full view of the public. An ample supply of grapes was displayed in the markets, of which our party secured a large quantity, which, with some of the dark, freshly baked bread, constituted a lunch, Tarsus having no hotel.

Camels, donkeys, and natives crowded the narrow and dingy streets. Evidently we were as great a curiosity to the people as they were to us, as we went through the principal streets in the quaintest of old-fashioned carriages. Droves of camels were arriving and departing, while many of these homely but faithful "ships of the desert" were lying in the shade, sheltered from the fierce rays of the ruddy sun, enjoying a brief though well earned rest.

St. Paul described Tarsus as "no mean city." Whatever may have been its character during his day

TARSUS.

it presented a squalid, unattractive, and positively mean appearance to us. For the first time we witnessed an Eastern khan, which was situated at this place. It had rooms to accommodate the men of the caravan, with an inclosed court and stalls for the animals below. In a similar spot at Bethlehem the Saviour was born, there being "no room" for the family "in the inn." Water, called by the Arab "the gift of God," is exceedingly scarce, and poor in quality. But seventeen inches of rain had fallen during the preceding year, which fully explains the shrunken appearance of the river Cydnus and the Falls of Cydnus, already described.

Before our train left Tarsus a visit was made to the traditional tomb of Sardanapalus and also to the Mohammedan mosque where the prophet Daniel is said to have been buried. The Armenian public school was in session, and fortunately we had the pleasure of seeing a group of bright-eyed little girls go out for a short walk under the direction of their teacher. Near by stood a plain Armenian church. According to tradition it is built on the site of the first Christian church in the city, the original foundations being utilized. Out of the ancient dome flew a large flock of fluttering swallows as we entered the venerable structure. Among other relics a piece of Noah's ark is soberly placed on exhibition. The men and women sit apart during hours of worship, occupying mats on the stone floor. The priest is permitted to marry but once, and in no case must he be united to a blood relative, under penalty of imprisonment for each offense. The Rev. Mr. McLaughlin, missionary, being away during the hot season, we were obliged to forego a visit to him which had been planned by some of the party.

Our next landing was Alexandretta, eighty miles distant. Before going ashore our hearts had been gladdened and our curiosity aroused by the appearance of the American flag, which was displayed above a large building near the sea-shore. It never seemed so beautiful before. We were unanimously of the opinion until we reached the spot that it must be the head-quarters of the United States consul.

It proved to be the licorice-root warehouse of the Stamford (Conn.) Manufacturing Company. Here was a genuine surprise indeed! Although seven thousand miles from home, we had stumbled upon the American flag, a Yankee business house, and a Connecticut one at that, owned by men residing only thirty miles from our family.

Mr. Daniel Walker, superintendent, courteously explained the operations of the company and gave us much interesting information regarding the condition of the country. The supply of licorice-root is obtained from the banks of the Euphrates, about three hours' ride distant. It is brought on the backs of camels in loads of five hundred pounds each. Apparently the supply is inexhaustible, as much of the root remains in the ground, which rapidly grows and spreads after the next rainfall. After being taken to the warehouse it is pressed into huge bales, bound with iron hoops, and conveyed by steamers to distant lands, where it is converted into licorice paste, such as is commonly seen in drug-stores.

Mr. Walker is a Scotchman by birth and has experienced many dangers and much rough usage among robbers, as he travels in this mountainous region to remote places in the interest of his business. However, he is as bold as a lion, and "none of these things move him." He goes well armed, is a good shot, and a superb horseman. He has the eye of an eagle, with the celerity and caution of a cat. In some combat in the near future he may fall, but the chances are that some of his foes will kiss the dust first. It is understood that he has already winged one or two deadly assassins who attempted his life.

But nominal wages are paid as a rule in this portion of the Turkish Empire. Mr. Walker stated that four and five cents a day was all that the natives received. Even blacksmiths were paid no more. The Stamford Company pays about fifty cents for a day's labor, which seems to the impoverished people a small fortune. Laborers will, with comparative ease, carry from four to five hundred pounds on their backs, about a camel's load. The Euphrates is the Mississippi or Nile of the region, furnishing in many ways much of the scanty employment to be found. The river is navigable for eleven hundred miles and is eighteen hundred miles in length.

From Alexandretta to Latakia the sail was eighty miles more. On the coast the spot is pointed out where Jonah was cast ashore by the fish that had swallowed him. Much of the entire coast-line is tame and uninteresting, though the exceedingly quiet sea and distant mountain ranges serve to render the trip a delight in other respects. We passed near battle-fields famous in history, where Alexander and Darius met in their memorable and deadly engagement, and near the line of march of the fanatical and undisciplined crusaders, together with many other noteworthy localities. After receiving more freight and passengers, spending a few hours, we hasten on. An attempt to land our party was abandoned, as the wily Turkish official wished to take all the passports with him, which would have caused a needless delay and served as a pretext for exacting additional and illegal fees.

Larnaca, on the Isle of Cyprus, seemed a beautiful place from the decks of our steamer. But long tramps over its hot roads, through beds of white dust which covered fields and travelers alike, speedily dispelled the pleasing illusion. Rude stone houses and walls of the eternal grayish-white reflected the merciless rays of the sun. Ever and anon a tall palm-tree nodded us a welcome, or huge cacti securely guarded groves of oranges and lemons from our presumptuous approach. At a wayside refreshment room forty cents were paid for two glasses of lemonade by members of our party within one hundred yards possibly of the spot where the lemons grew.

Since 1881 the island has been under British rule, and the Cross of St. George seemed a gratifying curiosity on the soil so long ground under the iron heel of Turkish misrule and oppression. Its acquisition by England was a pet measure of Lord Beaconsfield, and was accomplished during his premiership. Improvements already are inaugurated which will be indefinitely expanded in the near future. The natives do not take kindly to the change, and display a subdued restlessness in the matter. A vast amount of wheat was added to our already large cargo, besides a number of beef cattle. Ropes were fastened around the horns of the animals, by means of which the steam windlass hoisted them struggling on deck. Cyprus exports wheat, oats, barley, wine, oil, lemons, figs, olives, and cotton in moderate quantities. Its imports include a long line of "Yankee notions," besides flour, clothing, and hardware.

The island is cursed with fleas, sandflies, and locusts. Aromatic herbs, tobacco, silk, dye-woods, drugs, madder, fine qualities of wine, and a variety of fruits are easily produced. A long walk brought us to the cathedral, with no points of exceptional interest excepting an exhibition of the reputed grave of Lazarus. Since several other sites claim to hold his ashes, our enthusiasm was less pronounced than it might otherwise have been.

Tripoli loomed up before us on Sunday morning. Some of the party went ashore for two hours. It is fifty miles from Beyrut and about one hundred from Damascus. It has several mosques, orange groves, and produces a large quantity of silk, wood, tobacco, wax, soap, sponges, galls, and cochineal. Besides the cultivation of the soil, much attention is paid to fishing, the finny beauties being caught in an exceedingly primitive manner.

CHAPTER XI.

BEYRUT.—CAMPING TOUR BEGINS.—AMERICAN COLLEGE.—
FIRST NIGHT IN PALESTINE. — CHANGE OF PLAN. — MY
LONELY JAUNT TO JERUSALEM.

> "Thy river, O Kishon, is sweeping along
> Where Canaanite strove with Jehovah in vain,
> And thy torrents grew dark with the blood of the slain."

LATE on Sunday afternoon our steamer dropped anchor a mile off the shore in the beautiful harbor of Beyrut. As usual Turkish neglect had permitted the channel to fill up, while a mob of howling Arab boatmen climbed to the deck in pursuit of passengers. Since our arrangements had all been previously made, we were soon taken through a choppy sea which produced more nauseating symptoms than many days in mid-ocean had done.

Amid a babel of contending voices we wasted an hour in the custom-house while porters, boatmen, and other unwashed creatures thumped and pushed us in their mad rush for luggage and piastres.

Night closed in around us before we reached the comfortable New Hotel, kept by a kind, English-speaking Turkish landlord. He was clad in the national costume, as were all the servants. A royal dinner and a good night's rest closed our ocean trips for a season. Many regrets were expressed by members of our party that no time existed for visiting the celebrated American college and other noted

THE CAMPING TOUR.

places in Beyrut, since an eleven days' camping tour was to begin early the following morning.

Before leaving, however, personally, I had a brief interview with Dr. Bliss, president of the institution, whom I found to be a dignified, genial, and cultivated gentleman. The college is a grand success.

The camping tour at Beyrut began at an early hour. Long before the dawn of day a babel of voices was distinctly heard beneath our hotel windows, proceeding from Arab drivers, dragomen, and servants of various descriptions. Added to this were the pawing and stamping of fifty horses, with occasional whinneying from the poor beasts, which made it quite obvious that sleep for that night at least had "gone where the woodbine twineth."

Having from my boyhood been an early riser, seldom sleeping beyond four A. M., I at length arose, dressed, and packed my luggage for the long tour of eleven days that stretched out before us over hot roads and dizzy precipices. After a hasty breakfast the hour for starting arrived. With some delay, and a few mistakes, the tourists getting on to wrong horses, with a little jealousy on the part of one or two, who supposed that the best horses had been appropriated by other members of the party, we slowly wound our way out of the quaint old city of Beyrut. The long cavalcade of Protestant pilgrims presented, I dare say, a grotesque if not a bewildering appearance to the natives. Some of the party were exceedingly tall; others were less than medium height. One wore a linen duster, with a faded umbrella under his arm; a few had leggings, while one gentleman made the entire trip with a pocket handkerchief fluttering over his face and neck. To give my personal experience:

I had dreaded the camping feature for months prior to our departure from home. I knew nothing of horseback riding. A few times, when a boy, I had ridden a short distance on the back of the old farm horse. Now I am mounted on a spirited Arabian steed. Mr. Rolla Floyd, my personal and esteemed friend—the most noted dragoman in Palestine, who escorted General Grant and party during his memorable visit in Palestine—had chosen the best horse that could be had—a good walker and loper. The animals are all "tender bitted," we are told, so we must carry a slack rein. We are to speak to them in Arabic, but discover that learning the language during an exceptionally hot morning on the back of the brute are not the most favorable conditions under which the task might be accomplished. A faint, dizzy feeling crept over me, due in part to the half sea-sick condition produced while landing in the small Arab boat from the steamer the night previous, the lack of sleep, the heat of the morning, and my nervousness in learning to ride on the back of a strange Arabian horse. The caravan was out of sight, though we were still within the city. All efforts to guide the quadruped through the meager lesson given me proved fruitless. Feeling a decided disinclination to have eleven days of such a mockery for happiness while on a so-called "pleasure tour"—knowing that the intense heat would be almost unbearable at mid-day—I dismounted and decided to abandon the camping tour altogether. The

VIEW OF BEYRUT.

dragoman wished to fasten my horse to the one he rode, and so keep him with the caravan, but I declined peremptorily to go under any circumstances.

After sending word concerning my change of purpose to our party, I spent the day in visiting the bazaars and other points of interest in Beyrut, and sailed at five P. M. for Jaffa (ancient Joppa) by the

French steamer which brought us in the city the night previous. Mr. Rolla Floyd accompanied me. He resides at Jaffa, and I was to be his guest for three days.

The Presbyterian cemetery in the city contains the mortal remains of Bishop Calvin Kingsley, of the Methodist Episcopal Church. He died suddenly of disease of the heart while on an official tour to our foreign missionary fields, " wherever dispersed about the globe," April 16, 1870.

We reached Jaffa at sunrise the following morning. In a few moments, as if by magic, a flotilla of small boats surrounded the steamer, which fairly swarmed with bawling, swarthy, and gesticulating Arabs in pursuit of passengers. Though these steamers " book you " to Beyrut, Jaffa, and other ports, they anchor one and two miles from shore, and you are to land yourself on the best terms that can be made with these ravenous reptiles. Up the sides of the steamer they run like so many wharf-rats or Algerine pirates, hand over hand by any piece of rope that happens to hang from the vessel. One of them attempted it before some ship formality had been disposed of, when an officer of the steamer belabored the noisy, defiant fellow so lustily with a " rope's end " that he was glad to retreat to his boat.

The crew drew handspikes and the officers were

armed with various weapons as the comrades of the intruder made another attempt, and for a few moments it looked quite like a veritable battle with pirates. Finally the storm abated. The steamer party won. Permission was given when the red-tape

BISHOP KINGSLEY'S MONUMENT.

had been cut, and soon the vessel was alive with a swaggering mob of bullying boatmen, who seized luggage without permission and sought to compel passengers to accompany them to the shore.

A noisy crowd surrounded Mr. Rolla Floyd, yelling wildly for some time with clinched fists and swaying arms like so many murderous maniacs. At length, fearing my friend might be in some danger, not knowing what was said, as the language was Arabic, of which I could speak only a few words, I inquired :

"Mr. Floyd, what is the matter?"

"These boatmen," answered he, "say that this woman"—pointing to an intelligent and modest appearing lady near him—"has got to go with them in their boat, and if she does not go willingly that they will compel her to go. She has asked me to take her ashore in my boat, and does not want to go with them at all."

Plunging my hand into an inner pocket of my waistcoat I sprang before the mob, trying as much as possible to simulate indignation if not anger, and produced my passport. I had learned before that boldness was the only way to deal with an Arab. If you weaken either your cause, money, or life are at stake.

"Gentlemen," I shouted, sternly, "I am an American citizen. Do you see that," said I, pointing to the seal of the United States government and *visé* of the Turkish consul at Piræus.

"Yes," said one of them who understood English; "we do. It is a teschcaris," the Turkish term for passport.

"You are quite right." I answered; "it is a teschcaris, and I am," I repeated, "an American citizen. Now," I continued, making as much bluster as possible, "the first man among you that lays a hand on that woman must settle with me," jumping up and down and gesticulating wildly to impress them with my earnestness.

The words employed by me were translated into Arabic by one of their number, but with a strong amendment.

"This man," said he, as Mr. Floyd informed me later, "is an American, and he says that if any of you touch that woman he will have you put in jail within twenty-four hours."

Certainly this was an important addition, but the medicine proved efficacious. One by one, like the accusing Jews who wished to stone to death the trembling woman in the presence of Jesus, they scattered, until all were gone. Mr. Floyd conducted the lady, who was a teacher in a German school near Jerusalem, and myself to his residence in triumph. Since it had proved entirely too small to accommodate all the tourists who desired to board with him a few days in going to or from Jerusalem, he has been compelled to build the " Palestine Hotel" near by, where abundant room and an excellent table and bed are furnished at very low rates.

Mr. Floyd came to Jaffa with an American colony

SEA OF GALILEE.

of one hundred and fifty-three persons in 1866, organized under the direction of Bishop G. J. Adams, looking for the second coming of Christ. The date chosen, like thousands of others selected since the days of the apostles, proved delusive. Financial disaster at length overtook the colony; besides, the climate was oppressively hot for natives of Maine.

Subsequently, the entire property, consisting of some seventeen cottages, framed and prepared in Maine, was disposed of to a few thrifty and enterprising Germans, who still remain. Mr. Floyd alone is left of the original American colony, his residence being the same built by him in 1866.

Mr. Floyd has probably no equal in knowledge of Bible lands. The Rev. Dr. Theodore L. Cuyler, Joseph Cook, General Grant, Hon. S. S. Cox, and a long list of other noted travelers freely testify to this fact. He is a fine specimen of American manhood, and weighs fully two hundred and twenty-five pounds. Affable, obliging, and strictly honest in all his work, he is in great demand by American visitors especially. Dr. Cuyler freely declares that "Mr. Floyd knows every inch of the sacred soil better than any living man."

He is much crippled in his business by the narrowness of Turkish and of some United States officials, as well as by the friction of a rival tourist company.

The prompt dispersion of the mob on the French steamer, already described, was due in part doubtless to a wholesome lesson taught the imbecile and slowly dying Turkish government a few years ago by an American man-of-war.

A party of highwaymen attacked Mr. Floyd one dark night on a lonely road, demanding his money or his life. He was on horseback, armed only with a stout cudgel. His response was prompt and final. Quick as lightning he gave one ruffian a terrific blow on the head, and putting spurs to his horse escaped. The would-be robber and assassin fell to the earth. He was conveyed to his home by his confederates, and subsequently died from the effects of the blow given by Mr. Floyd in self-defense.

A brother of the dead man, undeterred by the well-deserved fate of his relative, determined to seek revenge and punish Mr. Floyd. So, waiting for a favorable opportunity, he came up secretly behind him and dealt his unsuspecting victim a severe blow upon the head with a club. Though partially stunned, Mr. Floyd quickly turned, when another blow aimed at his skull fell upon his shoulder. Grappling with his cowardly assailant, he threw him to the ground, giving him a severe beating, and tearing nearly all the clothes off of the desperado in the struggle. Now he turned him over to the dilatory Turk for punishment. Weeks, months even, passed, and yet to gratify some secret foes of Mr. Floyd the fellow was not brought to trial. Finally an American man-of-war chanced to enter the harbor of Jaffa while on an extensive cruise. Immediately a great consternation seized the minds of the local Turkish authorities. By some means the state of affairs and history of the case reached the captain of the American ship of war. He was prompt and resolute.

Donning his handsome uniform, he was rowed ashore, when he proceeded at once to the officials and informed them that " unless the assailant of Mr. Floyd was tried and sentenced within twenty-four hours he should proceed to shell the city."

New life characterized the action of the drowsy and snail-like officers of the Turkish government. Court was opened, witnesses examined, and before the sun sank below the waters of the blue Mediterranean the prisoner was pronounced guilty, fined $500, and sentenced to two years in jail, to remain until that amount was paid. Though sentence was immediately carried out, and the two years have long since elapsed, the culprit is still in jail, being wholly unable to pay the fine.

Of course, the action of the captain of the man-of-war was entirely illegal and unauthorized. Still, in coping with the crafty and tardy Turkish official the average American will rejoice over the result, even though done without adequate legal authority.

The heat of Jaffa was almost unbearable. A sirocco from the desert, like a furnace of fire, swept over Palestine a few days before our party arrived, making

A CARAVAN.

the atmosphere exceedingly oppressive to unacclimated Americans. Much of the summer, I was informed, the weather had been exceptionally cool. Of course, the camping party felt its full effects, though efforts were made to adopt the Oriental practice of starting very early in the morning before the sun had risen, and have long halts at camping places during the torrid mid-day heat.

Few objects of interest exist in Jaffa aside from the narrow streets crowded with camels and donkeys, the small, dingy bazaars, and the surging native population in their showy Oriental costume. The house of Simon the tanner is always visited, since the scene of the transaction described in Acts is situated at this place. Here the apostle Peter was tarrying when the divine command came to Cornelius, the centurion of the Italian band, "Send therefore to Joppa, and call hither Simon, whose surname is Peter; he is lodged in the house of one Simon a tanner by the sea-side: who, when he cometh, shall speak unto thee" (Acts 10. 32).

The building is a small one-story structure; but no one believes it to be the original house, though it probably occupies the same site. It has a flat roof with no wall to screen one from the gazers of the street, as in the prevailing style of architecture in the East. On the ground floor a mosque is located, which is never used during the time when tourists usually arrive, as their feet are supposed to defile the building, a tent near by meantime being used for a place of worship.

I visited the spot twice, the second time with the remainder of our party after the completion of the camping tour. Brief religious services were held on the top of the house, including prayer by the Rev. William Porteus, of St. Louis, closing with old "Coronation" and the benediction. Tanners still ply their trade in the neighborhood, and a stone vat at a nearby pump is believed to have been in use in St. Peter's day.

All attempts to drink the water evoked a determined and demonstrative resistance on the part of our stomachs. It was generally believed by us that the water was better adapted for tanning purposes, when the skins of dead animals are used, than to satisfy the thirst of American tourists, who come from a land proverbial for the purity of its springs and wells.

From Joppa Jonah fled before the face of the Lord when commanded to preach at Nineveh, as recorded in Jonah 1. 1–3: "Now the word of the Lord came unto Jonah son of Amittai, saying, Arise, go to Nineveh, that great city, and cry against it; for their wickedness is come up before me. But Jonah rose up to flee unto Tarshish from the presence of the Lord, and went down to Joppa; and he found a ship going to Tarshish: so he paid the fare thereof, and went down into it, to go with them unto Tarshish from the presence of the Lord."

In this city also Dorcas, that toiler for the poor,

was raised to life by St. Peter. Joppa, or Jaffa, is probably the oldest city on earth, having been built, in the opinion of very many scholars, long before either Damascus or Jerusalem. The city has been captured and pillaged three times—by Caliph Omar, A. D. 636; by the crusaders, A. D. 1090; and by Napoleon I., March, 1799. The story that Napoleon butchered three thousand eight hundred prisoners of war at this spot is regarded as apochryphal by competent and disinterested judges. An earthquake demolished the city in January, 1837, which resulted in the loss of thirteen thousand lives.

After three days spent at the delightful and hospitable home of Mr. Rolla Floyd I took a seat in an old-fashioned stage-coach for Jerusalem. It started at five P. M., and would not arrive at the Holy City until half-past seven o'clock the next morning. A dismal and lonely feeling pressed upon my spirits when I found that my traveling companions were all Arabs, who knew no word of English. They were apparently poor peasants, but civil and well behaved enough, however. Three horses were used, but the road, to my surprise, was a good one. After leaving Jaffa it was as smooth as a floor. Were it not for the white dust produced by the dry season the ride would have been much more of a satisfaction than it was.

A long line of orange groves is passed a mile or so after leaving the city. It is past sunset, and the deepening twilight makes the trees seem like ghosts or concealed robbers skulking behind the ugly and cheerless fence of cacti which serves to protect the precious fruit in some measure from the incursions of thieves. Had time permitted, a short ramble among the trees would have been pleasant, although the oranges would not reach maturity until December, two months later.

Vast plains many miles in extent lay before us, until at last we approached "the hill-country of Judea," where the Virgin Mary abode after the announcement made to her by the angel Gabriel concerning the birth of Jesus. It seemed a wild, desolate, rocky region, and, during the dry season especially, nearly destitute of trees or foliage. The route stretches across the immense plain of Sharon and through the historic valley of Ajalon.

Three stops were made to rest the horses between Jaffa and Jerusalem, ranging from one to two hours in duration. Some of the passengers took bedding from the stage, brought with them for the purpose, and lay down by the road-side while the halts were being made. Others wrapped themselves up in their abiah, or flowing striped cloak worn day and night throughout the year, and courted the god Morpheus.

Personally, I was wholly unable to keep warm, especially in the hours past midnight, when it was the coolest. All my luggage was on the backs of horses making the camping tour from Beyrut to Jerusalem, including my woolen tourist shirt and light overcoat. As the day was intensely hot when I began that journey so soon abandoned, as already related, I had divested myself of all underwear except a gauze shirt, wearing a thin summer coat, as my vest buttoned to my necktie. Vigorous efforts were consequently required to avoid taking cold. At the halting places, and also while the stage was creeping up the steep gradients of "the hill-country," I walked rapidly and swung my arms almost incessantly to keep the blood in circulation.

At one station a passenger in another stage bound in the same direction, also making a long midnight halt, called me by name. Astonished that any one seven thousand miles from home should know me, I responded. It proved to be a Mr. Brooks, of Stamford, Conn., who was making a journey around the world, and was joined at Cairo, Egypt, subsequently, by Mr. C. N. Crittenton, of New York city, one of our party. He had traveled from Smyrna to Beyrut with us, though independently, by the French steamer. It was two o'clock in the morning when we met.

Black coffee in cups holding not more than three or four thimblefuls was sold at a high price to the passengers in waiting. I ventured to accept a cup of

TOWER OF RAMLEH.

moiyeh, the Arab's term for water, which was offered me. It was so tepid and vile in taste and odor that I could only take a sip or two to wash the dust out of my throat. "Backsheesh," said the Arab, who stood before me in full Oriental costume. I had nothing smaller than a half franc, about ten cents, which I handed to him. "Thank you," he replied in fair English, and pocketed the coin. I reflected that from all indications dirty drinking-water was certainly held at a high price, and had my curiosity aroused to learn the commercial value of pure water.

One halt was at Ramleh, about twenty miles from Jerusalem, and another at Kirjath-jearim. The tower of Ramleh, built by the crusaders, is an object of interest. Expansive and extended views of that portion of the Holy Land are afforded from its summit in the day time.

On our journey we pass near the site of the five cities of the Philistines, visible from the tower— Ashdod, Gaza, Gath, Gimso, and Lydda. The scene of Samson's exploits is situated near our pathway, also where Dagon fell before the ark of God, besides the scene of David's duel with Goliath. Mount Carmel and other distant and noteworthy localities are also distinctly visible.

All through the long dreary night we passed long lines of camels laden with heavy burdens, including immense pieces of timber, long iron columns, and other severe loads. The poor, patient beasts carry them safely up and down the steep hills, and when they lie down on the journey the burden is not removed. Arabs, mounted on dwarfish donkeys, passed and repassed, also, as the night wore away, like so many wandering ghosts. The sky was cloudless, and myriads of stars twinkled in silent grandeur above us as we slowly wound our way among the solemn and majestic mountains to the far-famed city of Jerusalem.

CHAPTER XII.

Arrival at the Holy City.

First Impressions.—The American Family.—Sight-seeing Within and Around the Walls.—Gethsemane.—The Mount of Olives.—Bethany.—Bethlehem.—The Mosque of Omar.—Modern Buildings, Etc.

"If I forget thee, O Jerusalem, let my right hand forget its cunning. If I do not remember thee, let my tongue cleave to the roof of my mouth; if I prefer not Jerusalem above my chief joy."

MORNING finally dawned. Faint streaks of light in the east betokened the coming of the fiery god of day. We are nearing Jerusalem. Slowly we ascend the mountain that marks her western boundary. Now the blue mountains of Moab are distinctly seen on the distant horizon, feathery and dreamy, seemingly the happy home of some celestial poet or other favored inhabitant. Suddenly we are at Jerusalem, without the walls. Owing to our gradual ascent of the holy hill the view has been hidden and far less impressive than the approach from the east over the Mount of Olives. Modern buildings mostly are manifest, while others are in process of construction. The lumbering, dirty stage stops. A Turkish soldier from a sentry-box approaches us, and passports are in demand. Happily, mine is in my pocket, and not on the back of a packhorse with my luggage wandering over distant and dizzy precipices. It is critically examined. Since it is in due form, with a Turkish *visè* attached, there is no possibility for "backsheesh" to be wrung out of the sleepy and way-worn traveler.

Escorted by a guide I am conducted on foot through the Jaffa gate to the "American family," as it is called. No wheeled vehicles enter the walls of the Holy City, burdens and passengers being conveyed on the backs of donkeys and camels. Narrow streets are found, about the width of the average sidewalk, and yet destitute of separate pathway for pedestrians, while small dingy shops or bazaars abound. Little variety is found, as one must go to separate stores for nearly every article. In the streets, crowded with passing camels, donkeys, and pedestrians, the purchaser stands, or sits on his heels to select the goods. No one enters the small store or booth, as a rule, besides the proprietor or clerk. A very few establishments of recent origin are larger.

When the call for prayer is given from the minaret the Mohammedan merchant drops a netting down in front of his stock of goods, without locking or shutting doors, and goes away to worship. His bitterest enemy is not mean enough to molest any thing. If a customer chances to come and wishes an article of merchandise from his stock, the nearest merchant glances toward him and he leaves the money, taking the goods, the cash being undisturbed until the devout Mohammedan returns. Surely, here is primitive simplicity. It would be difficult to parallel it in Christian lands.

The "Americans," as they are styled, greeted me pleasantly, and stated with a genial welcome that "my room was ready for me." About eighteen or twenty persons are now included in this Christian home. Holding peculiar views possibly regarding the second coming of Christ, and the importance for some Christians, at least, to be at Jerusalem to illustrate his teachings by a godly life, they have for more than eight years walked by faith, and, like their divine Lord, go "about doing good." Jew, Gentile, Turk, or Arab are treated with equal courtesy. From limited resources they entertain frequent guests, never accepting payment, though offerings subsequently made for their missionary work are never declined. The loathsome lepers of the valley and sunny slopes of Jehoshaphat have received frequent and timely aid from them. Sick people, even those with small-pox, have been nursed by this devoted people back to health again.

A colony of one hundred and thirty poor Jews

THE MOSQUE OF OMAR.

recently arrived at Jerusalem, drawn, as they believed, by some inspired impulse suggesting the immediate restoration of their race. In their abject poverty the "Americans" provided for their wants. Armed Arabs from the desert have visited the "Americans" in a body and divested themselves voluntarily of their arms, which is never the case elsewhere in their intercourse with society. In return the "Americans" have accepted the hospitalities of the Bedouin, going long journeys under the protection of an armed escort furnished by the children of Ishmael. Then barbecues have followed, whole animals being stuffed with rice, cooked in an appetizing style, with a great variety of other Arabic dishes, while numerous servants sought to anticipate their every wish. After several days spent in this manner the family have been politely escorted to their home in Jerusalem, which is situated near the Damascus gate, and includes a portion of the northern wall of the city.

Turkish and American officials also visit them, as do many tourists from England, America, and other countries. Bishop Vincent during his recent tour became familiar with their work, being their guest for a short time. He has since recorded his impressions of them in the public press. It is inspiring in this degenerate age to see how much good a single family with a lofty purpose can achieve for suffering humanity, even under adverse circumstances. Death has thinned out their ranks since they first entered the Holy City. Mr. H. G. Spafford, author of the popular hymn, "It is Well with My Soul," was the leader of the movement. His widow is still a member of the household, and possesses a cultivated mind and a devoted Christian heart. The utmost harmony prevails in the family circle, all laboring to accomplish the greatest possible amount of good. One member of the family is a native of Boston, a Mr. Fuller. Though more than seventy years of age, he toils daily as a carpenter for the outside world, where his services are in demand, without accepting remuneration. Various articles are manufacture, such as chairs, bureaus, tables, etc., though no payment is demanded. Subsequent donations for their missionary operations, as we have already stated, are not declined. The family conduct divine worship daily at half-past ten A. M., which usually continues until noon. They are excellent singers, and their voices would be popular even in concert-halls, should they consent to sing in public. During my visit Professor Gilman, United States Consul at Jerusalem, and several Turkish officers took tea with them, and spent an evening in social intercourse.

With this devoted people I spent an entire week, while waiting for my party to come in from the camp ing tour to the Sea of Galilee, the Jordan, and elsewhere. Members of the family escorted me to all the prominent points of interest within and without the walls of Jerusalem. Mr. William H. Rudy, Mr. Herbert Drake, Mr. Page, and "Jacob" were exceedingly courteous and helpful in this particular. May the good work of this family long continue!

From Mr. Herbert Drake, a member of the "American family," the following communication was received about seven months after my arrival in the United States. Besides describing the primitive mode of harvesting the crops, it also shows that the grading of the long-talked-of railway, alluded to on another page, has finally begun, and furnishes much other interesting and valuable information:

"JERUSALEM, *June* 7, 1890.

"*To Rev. N. Hubbell:*

"DEAR SIR: It is a very late date to acknowledge and thank you for your kindness in sending to us the New York *Weekly Witness*, but, though late, we do thank you most heartily now.

"Perhaps it will interest you to know how things have been progressing in this city and country since your visit here in the fall. We have had a very good season, including a good later rain, which you may know is very necessary for a fruitful year. The market is accordingly now well stocked with different kinds of fruit and vegetables. These products seem to increase annually as more and more land is brought under cultivation. The Jaffa gate (the gate, you may remember, on the west side of the city, at the commencement of the Jaffa road) presents a very animated appearance in the early mornings at this time of the year, with the crowds of donkeys, fellaheen, etc., passing through laden with the products of the villages for the Jerusalem market. We are now, too, in the midst of grain harvest, which this year is exceptionally good. The wheat is cheaper this year than has been known for many years past. The country presents a fine sight now, with its extensive fields of ripe grain, looking very different from the view that met your eyes in the fall of the year. The instruments used for reaping are as primitive as those used in plowing. The same simple sickle is still seen as was probably employed in the time of the patriarchs, which is frequently mentioned in the Bible.

"It is a very pretty sight, however, to see the harvest reaped in this way. After it is cut, the grain is loaded on donkeys and taken off to the threshing-floors, where it is trodden out, as of old, by the foot of the ox or the ass.

"The wonderful movement among the Jews drawing them and attracting them toward their native land still continues. Jerusalem has just been visited by some rich and influential Jews (so we are told), the object of whose visit was to inspect and see if there was any favorable opening for additional Jewish colonization.

"There is at the present time a Jewish rabbi from Australia here, who is inspecting the Jewish colonies with a view to reporting on their condition in England and Australia, either encouraging or discouraging emigration of Jews to this country, according to the condition in which he finds them. These movements, even if they do not produce any direct immediate results, are yet in themselves indicators of an aroused feeling and desire awakened among the Jews scattered abroad toward the land of their forefathers.

"It was only quite lately that a large piece of land, capable, we were told, of maintaining four hundred families, was bought by the Jews near Jaffa. This piece lay between two other Jewish colonies, thus connecting them and forming with them one large tract.

"Some of the colonies seem to be rapidly progressing. In the colonies in the vicinity of Jaffa they say that there are three million vines planted by the Jews. We hear of a most extensive wine-cellar being built in one of the colonies at the present time at the cost of fifty thousand francs.

"In one of the colonies they have been planting out

VIA DOLOROSA.

this past season hundreds of mulberry-trees with a view to raising silk, and Baron Rothschild has also expressed a wish to have cotton raised.

"This possession and occupation by the Jews of the soil of their forefathers, and its reclamation from barrenness to fertility by their hands, speak loudly to us of our being on the threshold of a new time, spoken of both in the Old and New Testaments, the set time for the Lord to favor Zion, when the curse that has so long lain on both land and people is to be removed, and his blessing and favor again rest on them.

"Have you heard that the long-talked-of railroad has been at last commenced? The work was formally commenced on April 1. Up to the present time the force of workmen employed on the road has not been very great, but still some work has been accomplished. We hear of the engineers being busily occupied on their plans. The undertaking is in the hands of a French company. They have commenced operations from the Jaffa end of the road. The site for the depots at Jaffa and Jerusalem is kept a profound secret. Its commencement at the Jaffa end is north of the present high-road from Jaffa to Jerusalem. It crosses the road, perhaps, about half-way between Jaffa and the mountains, and continues from that point on the south side the whole of the remaining length of the plain.

"The valleys through which the railway is to ascend the mountainous country form a gradual ascent from the plain of Sharon to the level of Jerusalem, terminating in the plain of Rephaim. You will thus see that it will run close past the German colony, and the depot may be somewhere in the vicinity of the upper pool of Gihon; but, as I said before, this is kept a secret.

"Much work was done on the new Jericho road during the fall and winter. At times, it is said, there was a force of one thousand men at work on it. I dare say you remember enough of the country between Jerusalem and Jericho to understand that this would be a big job. One can now ride on a carriage out to Bethany, and I believe a piece of the road is completed at the Jericho end, but the sections between the two extremities are in a more or less unfinished condition, and there will be a good deal of work to be done yet before it is completed. They don't do this kind of work in the summer, partly, I suppose, on account of the heat, and partly because there is much work to be done by the peasants at home in connection with harvest, etc.

"In Jerusalem itself there is a good deal of building going on within the limits marked out in Jer. xxxi, 38–40, and Zech. xiv, 10. There are houses being built for Jews, and there is a scheme projected for building two hundred houses for Jews on the Montefiore property near the lower pool of Gihon on the west side of the city. One hundred of these will be for the Sephardim (Spanish Jews), and one hundred for the Ashkenazim (Polish Jews). There is preparation for considerable alteration and improvement in the Russian grounds and buildings. They intend providing accommodations more extensive than at present. They have made a grand entrance through the north wall of the old property, connecting this with the grand new hospice, and I hear they intend to make also a similar entrance on the south side, connecting the two with a drive. They also seem to be making preparations to enlarge the great French Catholic hospice on the north side of the city, or opposite the new Sultan gate.

"We mail you a few flower cards composed of flowers that we have picked ourselves in the fields around Jerusalem.

"Again thanking you for your kindness, and with our united love and best wishes, believe me to remain, Yours very truly,

"HERBERT DRAKE."

The chief attractions of the city and adjacent region were duly inspected long before the week expired when our party would return. They included the Mosque of Omar, "Robinson's Arch," the Via Dolorosa, the "wailing place of the Jews," the ruins of the hospital of the Knights of St. John, the Church of the Holy Sepulcher, besides missions, orphan asylums, synagogues, and minor mosques. A visit was also made to *Gehenna*, in the valley of Hinnom. Formerly children were here sacrificed to Moloch by backslidden Israelites. Later, constant fires were kept burning to consume the filth of Jerusalem conveyed to the spot. Long ages ago the fire was extinguished, and gloomy stone walls and a deep cellar remain.

A fanatic recently appeared and stated that God had revealed to him in a dream that the Ark of the Covenant was buried beneath the ruins. Permission was given him to make excavations. After much fruitless labor he abandoned the experiment in despair.

The celebration of the "Feast of Tabernacles" was in progress, which continues one week. It is designed to commemorate and delineate the mode of life practiced by the Israelites during their forty years' wanderings in the wilderness. Booths are erected in private yards, where the week is spent by the family occupying the premises. I was permitted to enter one of them. Services are also conducted at the synagogues, and on the closing day confectionery is distributed among the people.

At the "Tombs of the Kings" extensive catacombs,

burial vaults for deceased members of the royal family, exist. With the best preserved are stones showing how the door to the dead was anciently closed when the stone was rolled before it. The stone was as large as an average mill-stone, perfectly round at the edge, with flat sides, and rolled in a groove when

INTERIOR OF KING SOLOMON'S TEMPLE.

ample pressure was applied. A rostrum with a large inner court doubtless was the place where funeral services were conducted.

Gethsemane is undoubtedly wrongly located. It is at the base of the Mount of Olives, on the corner of two roads which were in use for centuries before the birth of Jesus, and are substantially unchanged in our day. It is also in full view of Jerusalem. Few can be induced to believe that so conspicuous a spot could have been chosen by the Saviour as a place of retirement and prayer. The fact that Judas was bribed to conduct the murderous mob of Jewish and Roman "hoodlums" to the place clearly indicates that it was in a much more isolated locality.

Eight old olive-trees are carefully fenced in by stone walls, while a variety of flowers and plants are cultivated within the inclosure by the aged Greek gardener. I visited the sacred site twice, both times alone. Here I read from my pocket Bible the description of the agony in the garden, the drops of blood, the sleeping disciples, and finally Judas guiding the mob and band of soldiers to the place. Though, like the Rev. Dr. W. M. Thomson and many more investigators, not wholly satisfied with the spot as the true locality, I could feel the solemn impressions suggested by the facts at least.

A new Greek church, not fully completed at the time of our visit, crowns the summit of the Mount of Olives. Its tall tower furnishes a fine view of this section of Palestine. I distinctly saw a portion of the Jordan as it empties into the Dead Sea, including a portion of this famous sea itself. A deep mist was rising from the Dead Sea as the waters evaporated beneath the fierce rays of the ruddy and scorching sun. The entire ascent of the tower, probably two hundred feet, is made by a stair-case only.

Bethany, the Mount of Olives, Gethsemane, Siloam, the brook Kedron, or its stony bed (for it is always dried up during the hot season, having no supply from springs, but surface-water merely), are before us. This little brook resembles the superficial and unstable professor of religion. Noisy and demonstrative during the rainy season, having no permanent spring as a source of supply, like the blighted fig-tree, it soon dries up. David knew a better way when he exclaimed, "all my springs are in Thee." So does the true Christian every-where.

The valley of Jehoshaphat; Jerusalem, with its venerable walls, minarets, the Mosque of Omar, the Tower of David, and other historical localities; also, more remote in the west, Bethlehem, the birthplace of Jesus; and far away the blue and majestic mountains of Moab, all are visible to the unaided eye.

Bethany, on a close inspection, proved to be practically a desolation. The foundation walls of the traditional house of Mary, Martha, and Lazarus, also of Simon the leper, where the scene of the transactions relative to the alabaster-box of ointment is laid, and a few Arab huts, comprise about all there is of interest. You must approach the place with a vast amount of religious sentiment if you desire any thing more.

MOHAMMEDANS WORSHIPING.

Desolate, stony, unfenced fields, devoid of grass, flower, fluttering leaf, or foliage of any description during the dry season alone are seen, except here and there a lonely dust-covered olive-tree, like so many sentinels guarding the place. The grave of Lazarus is pointed out, from which his resurrection took place. Cyprus and other localities claim to hold his ashes when death came to him the second time. Tradition asserts that Lazarus never smiled afterward when informed that he must die again after his resurrection. This, however, seems improbable, since the same divine power that had raised him once was ample to accomplish the pledge made—" Marvel not at this: for the hour is coming, in the which all that are in the graves shall hear his voice, and shall come forth " (John 5. 28). Martha declared that she " knew that her brother should rise again at the resurrection of the last day " —a fundamental fact freely and early taught the Jewish child by the dominant sect, the Pharisees. Millions of believers have since that day smiled at death when the hour of dissolution approached, in full hope of a glorious resurrection. Lazarus, then, having had the teaching of the wonderful Guest who honored his home with frequent visits, and who had summoned him back from the spirit world by his potent voice, could scarcely have regarded death with an exhibition of profound terror.

The entire region beyond Bethany, as you journey to the Jordan, is wild and desolate in the extreme. Save an occasional group of Arab huts, little of interest is visible. The fields are a mass of small stones, a bridle-path answering as a substitute for a road until the new and substantial one from Jerusalem, in process of construction at the time of our visit, is completed. Along the old road, meanwhile, your stumbling horse picks his way.

How changed is this treeless and verdureless section of the country since the days of Christ! Of course, the rainy season brings to life a myriad of tropical plants, flowers, and shrubbery, but the forests, through the action of war and the neglect and misrule of barbarians for weary centuries, have long since disappeared, together with much of the civilization which characterized the Romans and Jews.

By special invitation of the Arab sheik, sent through the "American family," I attended the celebration of three native weddings one evening at the village of Siloam. The place is directly east of and opposite to Jerusalem, near where the valley of the Kedron joins that of the Jehoshaphat.

It was a celebration rather than a marriage, as we understand the term. The marriage contract, in fact, is made by parents during the infancy of the children. On certain conditions, including a specified dowry, the agreement is made. Now a ratification is arranged, with a jubilee and a feast.

"Following my guide, and fearing no danger," I wended my way through the filthy streets of Jerusa-

THE HOLY SEPULCHER.

lem, with a horde of hungry and ferocious dogs at my heels. Out of St. Stephen's gate, down the steep and stony banks we descend, picking our way carefully among the dry bowlders in the bed of the Kedron.

The house of the sheik was dimly lighted. Through a dark and winding alley, up dangerous steps of stone, we groped cautiously till near the entrance; a feeble, flickering light indicated the location of the door. A bevy of demonstrative native dogs made the welkin ring as we approached. Though a wedding was in progress, the surroundings were needlessly dismal and unattractive.

We found the sheik to be a man apparently seventy-five years of age. He occupied a couch on the floor, being sick with "chills and fever," but arose as we entered, greeted us cordially, assigned me a divan, the seat of honor, and, apparently overcome with weariness, resumed his bed.

This was to be the home of one of the brides. Supplies had been secured for housekeeping, consisting in part of a stone bin of wheat, jars of olive-oil, and rugs and mats for bedding. All sleep on the floor, and no chairs, tables, or bedsteads are required. One Arab, who seemed to have charge of the festivities, was clad in a sheepskin coat, with the long white wool outside as originally worn by the animal. It was simply the pelt of the sheep, kept around his body by a girdle and some other security.

Finally refreshments were served. A large round metallic vessel was brought in, such as I had seen used on washing-day at Jerusalem. It was heaped full of boiled rice, over which some fat roast meat was placed, and was deposited on the floor in the center of the room. We were invited to draw near and partake, which we did, occupying a hassock instead of a chair. No plates, knives, forks, or spoons are required by the Arabs, since each one helps himself with his naked hands out of the single bowl or vessel on the floor. Small wooden spoons were considerately supplied the "American family" and myself, owing to our inexperience.

The importance of washing before and after meals, upon which so much stress is laid by both Jew and Mohammedan, was quite obvious. The latter never washes in a basin, lest dirty water should touch him and he be deemed ceremonially unclean. Water is therefore poured upon his hands by another, to avoid the difficulty, while he rubs them vigorously.

The Arabs, after we had been served, showed marvelous dexterity in plunging their hands into the boiled rice, compressing it into balls, and swallowing it with an obvious appetite, meanwhile making playful observations concerning our awkward manner of eating.

Finally the cry arose, "The bridegroom cometh." A motley group of people passed the house of the sheik in every conceivable style of dress and decoration, including native women, like wandering ghosts, with the inevitable white cloth covering their heads,

A BEDOUIN.

faces, and forms. A doleful and discordant drum was beaten, while a single taper, before which some one held an old hat to prevent it from being blown out by a gust of wind, lighted the procession.

We followed the merry-makers to an adjacent plaza which jutted out from the side of the mountain. Arabs in abiahs—a native cloak of camel's-hair, usually with black and white stripes—and in various styles of dress sat or reclined on the ground in the open air. A feeble fire glowed at the far side of the encampment, where black, muddy coffee was being made. It was served to all indiscriminately, with a cube of white sugar, but no milk.

Offerings of money were made from time to time in small amounts, with the understanding that the gross sum was to be divided equally between the three brides. An Arab with a stentorian voice announced the amount given and from whom, which kept up a monotonous din for an hour or two, adding, "Allah bless the giver." After a small contribution from me I heard the cry again, modified to suit the occasion, "Allah bless the A-mer-i-*can*," with a heavy and prolonged emphasis on the closing syllable. Later, one of the natives donated an additional contribution in my name, as a compliment, which evoked applause from the guests. Each couple arose to acknowledge the gift as the donations were called out, which gave them almost constant employment.

The marriage ceremony usually occurs at a very early age, while mere children, in fact, which seems very much like playing "keeping house" with a few dolls. One lady of the "American family," who, with others of that household, accompanied us, pointing to a young girl, said:

"That girl has been married two years, and I do not believe that she is more than ten years old now."

Just then the girl approached, and after an introduction to me the lady repeated the observation to her, and said, inquiringly:

"Let me see, you are ten years old, I believe."

"Indeed," responded the offended girl, quickly, "I am older than ten. I am *twelve*," with a heavy and unmistakable emphasis on twelve.

According to her own version, then, she was but ten years old at the time of her marriage.

Becoming chilled with the night air, as my heavier clothing was still on the back of a pack-horse among the mountains in the interior of Palestine, I was compelled to return to my lodgings at an early hour, though the marriage festivities usually continue in some form for three days.

A Jewish funeral procession wound its way along the eastern wall of Jerusalem and across the Kedron to the western slopes of the Mount of Olives, facing Jerusalem, as we returned. The body was "borne of four" on a bier. Perhaps four or five persons preceded it, bearing a lantern, others following. The Jews always bury at night. The dead body is regarded as ceremonially unclean, and receives slight

VIEW FROM THE WALL OF JERUSALEM.

consideration after death. As far as practicable all their dead are buried at the Mount of Olives, it being believed that in the morning of the general resurrection the dead of all the world must pass through the earth and rise at that locality. Wealthy Jews in many instances make provision for the burial of their bodies here, even when they die in distant lands. More than a century ago barks loaded with the bones of Jews, brought from distant ports, landed them at Joppa, whence they were transported on the backs of camels to Jerusalem for interment, for the reason already stated.

By very many it is believed that the restoration of the Jews to temporal power is near at hand. The decay of the Turkish Empire, the return of many Jews from other countries, the extensive new buildings now in process of construction within and without the walls of the city, the making for the first time in history of good, durable, and broad carriage-roads, with recent and repeated surveys for proposed railroads, the grading of which, according to recent dispatches, began shortly after our party sailed for America, point, in the judgment of very many, to important coming events. Block after block of modern stone structures are going up outside the walls, and many costly buildings are superseding old rookeries that have existed within the city from time immemorial. Three locomotives constructed in the United States have already been exported for the new Palestinian railway. They are named "Jaffa," "Ramleh," and "Jerusalem" respectively.

This prophecy, especially, certainly seems to be in process of fulfillment in our day, and great stress is laid upon it by resident Christians. The extent and direction of the new building, when taken into consideration, certainly seem to justify the cherished expectation:

"Behold, the days come, saith the Lord, that the city shall be built to the Lord from the tower of Hananeel unto the gate of the corner. And the measuring-line shall yet go forth over against it upon the hill Gareb, and shall compass about to Goath. And the whole valley of the dead bodies, and of the ashes, and all the fields unto the brook of Kedron, unto the corner of the horse gate toward the east, shall be holy unto the Lord; it shall not be plucked up, nor thrown down any more forever" (Jer. 31. 38–40).

"The ashes," or ash-heap, still remains outside the walls a little north of the Damascus gate. Here all the ashes which accumulated from the burnt sacrifices of the temple were deposited, since they were regarded as too sacred to be devoted to the purposes of fertilization. Alternate layers of broken stone have kept them in their place for centuries until recently. Now they are being carried away to be utilized in the new buildings in process of construction.

Lepers hover constantly about the traveler, begging. Even within the walls of the city, contrary to all law and precedent, a group of forty of them, at the ruins of the hospital of the Knights of St. John, made a rush for me one morning, and I was glad to escape from their contagious presence. Our party, however, before leaving Jerusalem made a cash contribution for their relief, which was left with "Joseph," the popular and trusty dragoman employed by Mr. Rollo Floyd.

After the return of our company we made a brief visit to Bethlehem. All the "sights" were seen, including the Church of the Nativity, the manger, and the various parts of the building, and near by the field where Ruth, the Moabitess, gleaned the fields of her kinsman Boaz, whom she subsequently married, and where in later centuries the angels appeared to the startled and sturdy shepherds as they announced the birth of Jesus. Our drive from Jerusalem to the ancient city was replete with interest, passing Rachel's tomb and other noted localities on the way. Darkness gathered around us before we had fully satisfied ourselves in seeing the prominent objects contained in Bethlehem. The touch of time and the wastings of war have, in a large degree, spared Bethlehem, and it remains essentially unchanged. Many of the people are engaged in the manufacture of mother-of-pearl breast-pins, the material being brought from the Red Sea. Some of the designs are very good; they include the dove, the camel, and the Star of Bethlehem.

Ages have glided swiftly away since the star-guided magi journeyed from the remote sands of

Arabia in pursuit of this mysterious nocturnal visitor. The wise men now slumber in unknown graves. The startled shepherds with their peaceful flocks have vanished from the rugged mountain slopes of Judea. The mighty power of the Roman Empire is broken.

A JERUSALEM JEW.

The imperial throne of the Cæsars is vacant. The glory of Greece has departed. Earth's monarchs who then swayed the scepter, with their dauntless cohorts and legions, have long since moldered to their native dust. The prince and the peasant, the beasts that roamed the ancient forests, the fish that sported in the sea, or the song-birds that warbled in the tree-tops—all are gone. But Jesus, the Son of Mary and the Son of God, still reigns. According to his prediction, he is drawing all men unto himself. The uncounted millions of China and Japan have heard the glad tidings. Korea is to be redeemed. The deep and awful lethargy of India is lifting. Africa, too, has been invaded by the intrepid and enthusiastic Bishop William Taylor and his noble band, while the isles of the ocean have caught a glimpse of this wonderful midnight star, and rejoice in its God-given light.

It is a significant fact that the wealth, railways, commerce, inventions, science, and literature of the globe are chiefly in the hands of Christian nations. The Methodist Episcopal Church alone builds two new houses of worship daily for the Master, while a million of souls throughout the world are annually converted to God.

Radical changes in the mode of observing Christmas have, indeed, been made since the rude period when

> "The mistletoe hung in the great castle hall,
> And the holly branch shone on the old oak wall."

The huge wassail bowl of punch has largely been supplanted by the less stimulating beverages of tea and coffee. The crackling yule-log has vanished before the glowing anthracite. The boar's head has been supplanted by the far-famed turkey. The excited chase and the huntsman's horn have yielded to the mellow tones of the Sabbath-school bell. Myriads of children in neat attire, with their parents and friends, annually commemorate the season with gospel songs and scriptural recitations at the house of God.

The term Christmas being derived from the Latin words, *Christi-Massa,* denoting the mass of Christ, should by all means be religiously observed. It is the birthday of the Prince of Peace. The day should not be devoted exclusively to feasting and the bestowal or reception of gifts Let each human heart be given fully and irrevocably to Him. Acts of charity should, indeed, be numerous and multiform. Heal estrangements and banish hideous hate by the benign principle of love. Not for the day merely, but for all time. Alas! it often occurs that

> "We ring the bells and we raise the strain,
>   We hang up garlands every-where,
>   And bid the tapers twinkle fair.
>   Feast and frolic, and then we go
> Back to the same old lives again."

CHAPTER XIII.

KING SOLOMON'S FAMOUS MARBLE QUARRY.—ON TO EGYPT.
—THE SUEZ CANAL.—EGYPTIAN MOSQUES AND WOMEN.
—A VISIT TO THE SPHINX AND PYRAMIDS.—THE HOWLING
DERVISHES.

> " The traveler owns the grateful sense
> Of sweetness near, he knows not whence,
> And pausing takes with forehead bare
> The benediction of the air."—*Whittier*.

PREVIOUS to our departure from Jerusalem we visited the famous marble quarry of King Solomon. It is a vast subterranean vault, being situated immediately beneath the time-honored and sacred metropolis. Entrance is made outside the walls near the Damascus gate. Many tourists and even some permanent residents are entirely ignorant of its existence. From this spot all the marble was taken which was used in the construction of Solomon's Temple.

The cave is of great extent. It extends in various directions, one corridor leading nearly half way to the former site of Solomon's Temple, where the Mosque of Omar now stands. The marble is of great purity and as white as snow. This justifies the traditional observation attributed to the Queen of Sheba during her memorable visit to Solomon, as she marveled at its silvery whiteness glistening beneath the brilliant rays of an Oriental sun. The foundation walls of the temple, composed of massive blocks of hewn stone, still stand, and are shown to visitors, descent being made for fifty feet, perhaps, below the outer soil, where the *débris* of centuries conceals the marvelous masonry from the superficial observer. They were laid 1000 B. C., and were furnished by Hiram, King of Tyre, as described in 1 Kings 5. 17. The marble, however, was found on the very spot. The site is the ancient threshing-floor purchased by King David of Araunah the Jebusite for fifty shekels of silver, as a place of sacrifice to stay the ravages of the plague, which had already swept away more than seventy thousand of his subjects.

Marks of the tools, wedges, and other implements used in removing the immense blocks of marble are plainly visible on the walls and roof of the quarry. Even the lamp-black from the primitive lamps employed by the workmen, which were inserted in crevices of the rock, still remains. No one doubts that the quantity of marble removed furnished an ample supply for the completion of the world-renowned temple of King Solomon. Apparently, an unlimited quantity of this excellent material still remains, which may ere long be needed if modern buildings shall

ON TO EGYPT.

continue to be erected at Jerusalem in the future as during recent years.

Beneath the ancient city abundant evidence remains to confirm the remarkable biblical statement that "there was neither hammer nor ax nor any tool of iron heard" when the temple was being built (1 Kings 6. 7). Below the bustle of the narrow and crowded streets of Jerusalem skilled workmen, like so many coral insects beneath the tumult of the ocean, noiselessly and industriously labored on until the stupendous superstructure was completed. Then their secret toil was seen and appreciated by the countless thousands who gathered at the royal palace, as the work of the humble Christian laborer will be at the judgment day.

The days of Turkish misrule, happily, are nearing the end. Hopelessly bankrupt, unable either to clothe or pay her soldiers, pursuing ceaselessly her dog-in-the-manger policy, the climax cannot be far distant. Who will secure the prize when the fruit falls, as fall it must? Shall England, France, Germany, or Russia? No one can with absolute safety predict. If native sentiment were a factor in the solution of the problem England would *not* gain the coveted land. For some cause the people of Palestine would prefer almost any other nation to her. Russia would be their choice if it were clearly expressed. However, the judgment of a mongrel and semi-barbarous people will be of small significance when the clash of arms resounds throughout the Orient, if not in large portions of Europe itself.

On every hand the influence and work of Russia can be distinctly traced. New Greek churches are being completed within and without the walls of the Holy City, besides extensive blocks of modern dwellings, stores, and other structures. The famous and venerable ruin, the hospital of the Knights of St. John, Russia especially covets. It was presented to Germany by the Turkish government. "Name your price and you shall have the sum," says Russia. "We need it for our church; you do not. It is near the Church of the Holy Sepulcher, hence almost indispensable to us." Thus far the blandishments of Russia have been successfully resisted by the sturdy German. Doubtless the sword will again be required to cut the Gordian knot. The building was erected by the crusaders.

From the days of Abraham to those of Disraeli the hunted Hebrew has engaged the attention of mankind to an extraordinary degree. The history of this ancient and peculiar people covers an eventful and interesting period of nearly four thousand years. Since his migration from Egypt the Jew has been alternately a *protégé* of Providence, devout or idolatrous, and in all ages the victim of cruel and intolerable oppression. A homeless fugitive, banished by unjust edicts from many ruling monarchs, his property confiscated, personally ostracised, traduced, imprisoned, and tortured, he has preserved in all lands the Old Testament, the Talmud, the Targum, his language, religion, and national characteristics.

At the taking of Jerusalem by Titus, A. D. 70, no fewer than one million one hundred thousand Jews miserably perished. Sixty-five years later five hundred and eighty thousand more were also butchered by the infuriated Romans. Even in England multitudes of the race were brutally massacred at London, in 1189, at the coronation of Richard I. Five hundred unhappy Jews shut up in York Castle and menaced by a murderous mob, in 1190, unable to escape, mutually cut each other's throats. King John, in 1204, put to death vast numbers of both sexes, and chiefly for his personal amusement extracted the teeth and plucked out the eyes of many more. In 1262, at London, seven hundred Jews were put to death for usury, and in 1278 two hundred and sixty-seven others were hanged and quartered on the charge of mutilating coin. During the year 1290 the Jews, fifteen thousand six hundred and sixty in number, were formally banished from England, and were not permitted to return until the rule of Cromwell three hundred and sixty-seven years afterward.

The struggle of the Jew for the attainment of his civil and political rights was prolonged, and became proverbial. During a period of nine consecutive years Baron Lionel de Rothschild was thrice elected member of Parliament by vast majorities before permission was granted him to take his seat. In Russia, Austria, Spain, Portugal, France, and elsewhere the contest was protracted and bitter, but, happily, of a less sanguinary character. The dark cloud of prejudice has measurably lifted, and under the benign influences of Messiah's reign—the Prince of Peace—it is fervently hoped, will speedily disappear forever.

In all the departments of commerce, literature, music, the fine arts, and scientific research the Jew has amassed wealth and achieved an enviable distinction, even "Amid the world's reproach and cruel victor's scorn."

His Bible, describing the deeds of such renowned Hebrews as Abraham, Joseph, Moses, Joshua, David, Solomon, Daniel, Isaiah, and Jeremiah, is our Bible also. The four evangelists, together with Paul, and Jesus the son of Mary and the Son of God, were likewise Jews. Persecution with fire and sword, the dungeon, the rack, and the cross have vanished like some hideous nightmare. The hunt for Hebrew souls

"SEE NOW, I DWELL IN AN HOUSE OF CEDAR, BUT THE ARK OF GOD DWELLETH WITHIN CURTAINS."

has happily begun. May multitudes of God's chosen people be captured by the "Galilean King!" Grander results than attended the enthusiastic but unfortunate crusade of Peter the Hermit will yet be witnessed. "The lost sheep of the house of Israel" are coming to Jesus, of whom "Moses in the law and the prophets did write."

The Jewish mission recently inaugurated in New York by the Rev. Jacob Freshman, a faithful Christian son of Abraham, not to speak of flourishing organizations in other portions of the United States, is meeting with encouraging success, and deserves the hearty and substantial sympathy of all Christians every-where. The day dawneth! Night flees apace!

A rapid ride by daylight, with the members of our party, from Jerusalem to Jaffa, was exceedingly enjoyable. Though the route was the same previously traveled by us during the night, we were enabled to see objects of interest afresh and to better advantage. The night was pleasantly spent at the new and comfortable Palestine Hotel, Jaffa, owned by that prince of dragomans, Mr. Rolla Floyd.

In the morning another ramble was taken among the bazaars, including a second visit to "the house of Simon the tanner." A few of the party took short rides on the backs of camels, led by their Arab owners, which involved a fresh outlay of "backsheesh."

After a farewell dinner in the "Land of Promise" we make our way through the narrow streets to the French steamer which is to convey us to Port Said, Egypt, the gateway to the famous Suez Canal. Arabs in coarse striped camel's-hair cloaks—termed abiahs—with hordes of donkeys and camels, crowd the streets. Porters with huge boxes on their backs, strapped to their heads and chests, almost a load for a horse, block up the way.

As we bid a long and possibly a lasting farewell to Palestine, the words of Whittier seem expressive of our closing impressions:

> "O, the outward hath gone! but in glory and power
> The spirit surviveth the things of an hour."

In the gray dawn of an October morning anchor is dropped at Port Said, which presents a quiet and modern appearance. The completion of the Suez Canal to this point, where the waters of the Red Sea and the blue Mediterranean were united, gave it some degree of prominence. English names appear on the public signs, with a larger proportion in the Arabic and Greek language. Our stay is necessarily brief. Embarking on a cockle-shell of a steamer, we sail down the famous canal to Ismailia, where a grand dinner awaits us, as well as an Egyptian railway train to convey us to Cairo.

Some conception of the formidable character of the work performed by De Lesseps can be inferred as we sail on for hours beneath the relentless and scorching rays of an African sun. The width of the excavation varies from one hundred and twenty to three hundred feet, besides extensive docks and harbors for

ON THE SUEZ CANAL.

the repair and temporary anchorage of vessels on their way to distant lands.

Hundreds of camels urged by Arab drivers were busy at one point conveying loads of sand in sacks on their backs to the top of a steep inclined plane, the object being evidently to widen the canal for some local purpose at that particular spot.

From the steam-boat landing at Ismailia to the railway depot the roadway is lined with the carob-tree. It produces the "husks" fed to the swine, or pods somewhat resembling beans, coveted so eagerly by the prodigal son in his migrations from the paternal mansion. Tradition also declares that John the Baptist used it likewise as a portion of his frugal *ménu*. The tree affords abundant shade, and at the time of our arrival was laden with the long pods, presenting a graceful picture. Several members of the party secured specimens to exhibit to the children of their respective Sunday-schools.

The ride to Cairo proved a positive delight and surprise in some respects. Coming, as we did, from the arid and ashen desolation of Palestine, where vegetation, deprived of water for several months, was seemingly extinct, naught but heated limestone and dust being visible, Egypt blushed in verdant beauty like the very Garden of Eden. On every hand an abundant harvest was manifest. Limitless fields of wheat and Indian corn—with cotton and other crops—stretched far away in the distance. Even now, as in the days of Joseph, there is a measureless supply of "corn in Egypt." For weary weeks no green thing had been witnessed in our travels throughout Europe and Palestine, save the dust-covered olive, fig, and a sprinkling of other tropical trees. How marvelous the change!

The secret of it all was the Nile. Irrigation here is a pronounced success. It reminded us of the famous painting at the Vatican, Rome, where the Nile is symbolized by a female with children in her arms and various animals at her feet, with fruits, vegetables, and other native products, denoting the unlimited supply which she bestows upon man and beast.

In the way-side fields grazed peacefully the African buffalo, and occasionally the camel, with flocks of large black goats and sheep. The date-palm laden with luscious fruit lifted its lofty form on high, as if conscious of being an important, if not indispensable, contributor to the public good. Low and squatty houses of sun-baked brick were common. Their mean appearance seemed utterly out of harmony with the prodigality and grandeur of nature which surrounded them.

The road-bed of the railway was in bad repair. Such swaying of cars, bouncing, and discomfort had been nowhere else experienced. To add to the misery blinding clouds of dust literally covered the miserable pilgrims. All things finally end, and so did the journey to Cairo. Thorough ablutions, a substantial *table d'hôte* dinner at seven P. M., followed by refreshing sleep, prepared us in some degree for the duties of the succeeding day.

The Boulak Museum of Egyptian curiosities and

antiques presented few novelties to those who had witnessed similar displays at the British Museum, London, and at various points in New York city. The mummies of Rameses II., who flourished contemporary with Moses, and other Egyptian monarchs were included in the collection.

On a Nile boat, adjoining the exhibition, was being loaded a huge stone statue of the Pharaoh of the exodus, the tyrant task-master and pursuer, whose fierce forces met with so overwhelming a defeat in the Red Sea during the career of Moses. Apparently, the huge block would weigh fully one ton. Yet it was fastened to a series of poles placed on the shoulders of perhaps a score of dusky and stalwart Arabs and Nubians, being carried along slowly, while all joined in a cheery chorus which sounded like "Allah is great; Allah is great." The image was to be transported to another locality on the Nile, to embellish a public garden.

Women in Egypt, as in other Mohammedan countries, conceal their faces by ugly veils of black or variegated hues, according to their age, but unlike other lands, expose the eyes and a portion of the forehead. A brass or wooden cylinder about the size of a spool of thread is displayed on the forehead. This is for the purpose of concealing the tape fastening the veil to their heads, and possesses no religious signification, as many mistakenly suppose. Hordes of donkey boys make one's life miserable by incessantly dogging your footsteps around the city, crying in fair broken English, "Donkey, sir; very goot donkey." You pause at a bazaar window to inspect an article therein displayed, or to see some object across the street, but

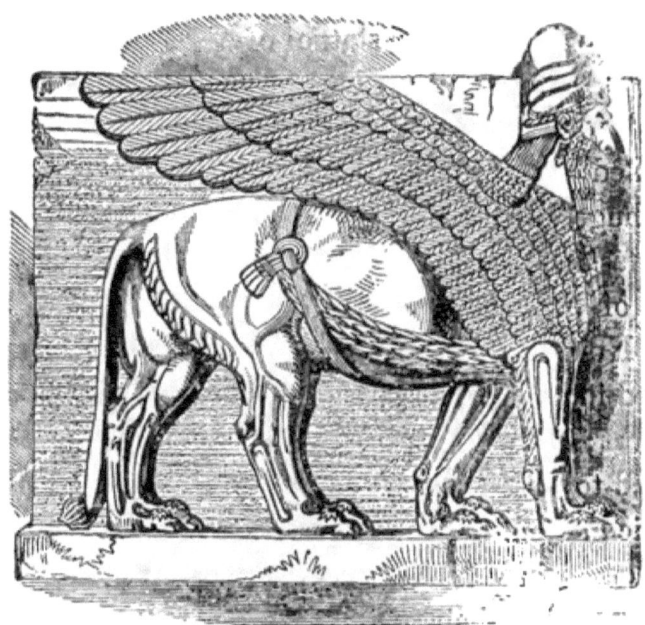

THE WINGED LION.

the everlasting din of "Donkey, sir," goes on. Even when our entire Palestine party have just taken a long line of carriages for a distant drive the clamor continues, though it should be obvious, even to an Egyptian donkey boy, that a traveler cannot be in two remote places at once nor ride two quadrupeds at the same moment, especially if going in opposite directions, unless he chances to be a professional politician or a clerical mountebank.

Not unfrequently, in order to secure the patronage of the traveler, he names his animals for the time being after well-known personages in the country where he presumes the visitor came from. Hence, to American travelers, he cries: "Here is your Mark Twain donkey, Mary Anderson donkey, or Grover Cleveland donkey." To the Englishman he shouts: "Here is your nice Gladstone donkey, and Queen Victoria donkey, with two beautiful black eyes."

Various mosques about Cairo were duly visited. One morning in particular we removed our shoes three times to enable us to enter these structures, a peculiar sanctity being attached to the spot. While visiting the Mosque of Omar, at Jerusalem, one of the party thoughtlessly expectorated on the floor. Our Mohammedan guide immediately threw himself on his knees, bowed his head to the floor, and kissed the very spot to purify the premises. The interpreter absolutely declined to translate the personal epithet applied by the devotee to the thoughtless offender, lest a religious outbreak should occur. It might serve as a lesson to Christian worshipers every-where, at least, to preserve their places of worship from

THE PYRAMIDS.

desecration and defilement as far as is consistently practicable.

The Mosque of Mohammed Ali is the handsomest and costliest structure of the Mohammedan faith at Cairo, unsurpassed even by the renowned Mosque of St. Sophia, Constantinople. The architecture is exceedingly grand and imposing. Much of the outer and inner walls are composed of solid alabaster. Within, costly mosaics adorn the building, while precious stones of many attractive colors shone resplendently in the beautiful dome. Various worshipers were at prayer in portions of the building. "The dim religious light" and the murmur of distant voices at devotion produced sensations of an impressive character. Costly Turkish carpets of tasteful patterns, thick and soft, covered the floor. Their cash valuation, aside from the associations attached to them, would doubtless have exceeded $50,000. Experts, indeed, have made an estimate approximating that sum.

The tombs of the kings of Egypt were also grand, and well deserve a visit. Millions of dollars were expended upon these beautifully decorated sarcophagi to commemorate the name and fame of ancient and terrible tyrants. Among the most modern of them was one containing the body of the mother of the present Khedive of Egypt. It was a sculptural gem of rare and exquisite beauty.

Included in the list of strange sights in Cairo should be mentioned the presence of women in the streets, with broad shallow baskets poised on their heads, picking up the animal droppings with their naked hands and placing them in the baskets. Here, there, and yonder they dart, absorbed in their lowly though disgusting labor, never removing the basket or spilling its contents. The accumulation is conveyed carefully to their humble homes, where it is dried for fuel. Owing to the utter absence of forests or woodland of any description in the country, save the stumps and roots of decayed fruit-trees, and an occasional branch brought down by the Nile, the problem of fuel proves a startling one.

A superb carriage ride led from Cairo to the pyramids and sphinx at Ghizeh. Much of the way the road was well shaded from the fierce rays of the blazing sun by a long line of tropical trees. The roadway ran along various local branches of the wonderful Nile, the main stream being crossed by a bridge. Little evidence of commerce was visible on its waters. A few small sailing-vessels with tall curved masts alone lent animation to the scene. The ascent of the pyramids was made by some of our party, while a few entered the gloomy pile of stones to visit the burial chambers of the king and queen. Others were quite content to view the wonderful monuments from the surface of the earth, and endeavor to realize the fact, stated by Napoleon during his campaign here, that "forty centuries looked down upon them." But little opportunity for reflection was possible, owing to the small army of guides proffering their services, or Arabs with antiques to sell or camels to let for a

THE SPHINX.

short drive. Though the average tourist is hunted by beggars and peddlers daily through many lands, yet the climax is reached at the pyramids. To decline politely a dozen times means nothing to the Arab or Egyptian. Nothing less than bluster, with the appearance of terrific rage, finally drives them away.

Personally, I declined all invitations to ascend the pyramid or to enter its dark and dismal vaults. However, in a moment of exuberant good-nature, for a trifling service I presented the Arab sheik with my pocket-knife. Arab like, he wished to show his gratitude and extend to me some rude hospitality. Hence moiyeh (water) in a stone jar was repeatedly urged upon me. Knowing how sensitive the race is concerning refusals of such courtesies, after much coaxing on his part I consented to be shown the interior of the pyramid.

He called three stalwart natives, who seized me by each hand, alternately pulling or pushing, and I was hurried into the grim grave of forgotten kings. The descent was rapid, being an inclined plane of marble worn as smooth as glass by constant use, since pilgrims have gathered here from all climes during the past four thousand years. At some points I was compelled to crawl on my hands and knees through a small hole; elsewhere, the three sturdy Arabs lifted me almost by main strength over a wall nearly as high as my head. Finally we reached the "Queen's Chamber," where we shouted and clapped our hands to hear the echo from the vaulted ceiling.

The well in the interior was pointed out, and a swarthy Arab offered to go to the bottom of it with a light if I desired it, which I declined with thanks.

Now the men made a demand on me for "three good backsheesh," meaning a large present to each man for escorting me. Knowing that the conductor of our party had paid the sheik for the entire company, and that I was the guest of the sheik himself, who desired to show me a courtesy for my small present, I positively declined to contribute a single piaster.

I was alone in the center of the great pyramid of Ghizeh. The men might be cut-throats or desperadoes of some description. Be it as it may, I had firmly resolved to make no payment on principle when the journey began, even at the risk of my life. It is a common trick of the natives to get the traveler half way up the pyramid and extort more money from him, threatening to push him down, or within the gloomy and ghostly tomb make a similar demand at a lonely and dangerous point.

Springing quickly back, and assuming an indignant if not a hostile attitude, I shouted, lustily:

"Not one piaster! I am here as the guest of the sheik. Let no man lay hands on me to resist me. No further will I go. Back to the open air I will find my way alone. I will report every man to the sheik."

The effect was almost magical. Like whipped spaniels they fawned around me.

"We no want backsheesh. You will please no tell the sheik. We are your servants. Let us show you the King's Chamber."

"No," I answered; "not another step will I go with you. I am the guest of the sheik. He shall hear of it, and I will return alone. Hands off, every one of you."

I returned, but in spite of all my opposition they persisted in rendering me some assistance, occasionally ejaculating:

"We are your servants. You will please not tell the sheik."

I was glad enough to reach the open air once more, but failed in my attempt to report them to the sheik. Mistaking another Arab for him, I told the story. He did not understand many words, and laughed loudly. Seeing my mistake, I tried to speak to the real sheik alone, but found it impossible with so many natives and tourists around him, and was compelled to abandon the idea. One of my three Arab guides came crouching around me just as our carriage departed for Cairo, making a final attempt for money. It proved fruitless, however.

"Vatever you please," he continued, when I again refused.

"I *please* to give you *nothing*," I added, sternly. And with a subdued look on his hangdog counte-

ENTRANCE TO THE GREAT PYRAMID.

nance, he at length disappeared in the deepening shadows of the evening while we drove on.

"Egyptian darkness" indeed closed in around us before our party reached the hotel at Cairo. My carriage, containing four besides myself, two of whom were ladies, members of the company, had very poor and slow horses. No amount of whipping could induce them to proceed faster than a walk. Twice guides came back to look for us. Finally, as we were then three or four miles from our destination, another carriage was procured, and we were driven rapidly to the hotel.

The sphinx, it should be remembered, was worshiped as one of their gods by the ancient Egyptians. The design was undoubtedly that its sleepless eye might watch over the dust of the departed monarchs slumbering in the adjacent pyramids. It is cut out of solid rock. Possibly it served also as a solemn symbol of immortality, the watchful and far-away look denoting unbroken interest in human affairs as well as continued existence of conscious being.

No one should leave Cairo without visiting the howling dervishes. They meet for worship every Friday afternoon at two o'clock. Though our train for Alexandria departed at four P. M., we managed to spend about an hour among this peculiar, small, and fanatical sect. Their religion was brought from Persia, and presents many curious and grotesque peculiarities as observed by its zealous and demonstrative devotees.

All are seated in a circle on the floor of a mosque of a plain and unadorned description. The mellow notes of a flute are heard, and each person joins in a succession of snorts and grunts, sometimes barking like a dog or puffing loudly like a locomotive. An Ethiopian, in a white turban and a sort of surplice, enters, bearing a wand, and performs some astonishing swirling with outstretched arms. Round and round he goes, while the puffing and snorting go on, but with new sounds ever and anon. Nearly all are swaying and rocking from side to side, or backward and forward. Two or three gain their feet, swinging themselves wildly to and fro, the long black hair of one flying in the breeze, making him look like a veritable witch astride of a broomstick. A dignified old man keeps them in proper position. Any deviation from the prescribed rule involves a mark of disapprobation or some sort of a penalty. The great effort is to mortify the flesh by laboring even to downright exhaustion. If one falls prostrate from an attack of vertigo, or in an epileptic fit, it is deemed a signal success, but the weary work still proceeds with renewed vigor. At Cairo the sect is small and barely tolerated by the government. Constantinople furnishes greater facilities for their work, and nowhere outside of Persia can the howling or whirling dervish be studied to greater advantage.

Cairo is both old and modern. The most ancient portion of the city was begun A. D. 638. The population is well-nigh cosmopolitan. Arabs in their abiahs, or coarse cloaks, with bare, dirty legs, and children entirely nude, crowd the streets among stylish and dainty ladies and gentlemen from remote portions of Europe and America, or possibly well-to-do and permanent native residents. Donkeys and camels crowd the streets. A modern traveler describes his observations as follows:

"Dragomans, black, yellow, and white, splendidly dressed in flowing trousers, silk and satin vests, embroidered jackets, and immense turbans, are quarreling with donkey owners, who are finding fault with donkey drivers, who are doing the same with the donkeys. The traveler threatens to belabor the dragoman, the dragoman does belabor the owner, the owner belabors the boy, and the boy the donkey, and none of them seem to care much for it. Add to this a half dozen mountebanks, a dozen dealers in relics, turbans, and handkerchiefs, fifty dogs, one of whom is playing circus with a monkey on his back, a snake-charmer with a bagful of snakes all standing erect, if a snake

HIEROGLYPHICS.

can stand, with fangs protruding, ready to make a plunge at their conqueror, who offers to swallow any one of them for a shilling, and you have a faint idea of what is going on daily in the city."

Alexandria, distant from Cairo one hundred and thirty miles, was reached in about four hours. Rapid traveling is not one of the besetting sins of the Egyptian railway. Unless the road-bed were placed in better repair it might prove an "upsetting sin," as a colored brother once described the vice of intoxication. Its broad plazas, fine public buildings, pleasant streets, and comfortable hotels will long be held in cheerful remembrance. It is the sea-port and commercial capital of Egypt. During the summer it is the official residence of the khedive, who removes to Cairo in the fall. His return was daily expected when we left, and public buildings and the main thoroughfares were profusely decorated with bunting, palm branches, and other forms of adornment. He is more popular than many of his predecessors. The presence of an English garrison at Cairo and Alexandria elicits but little complaint, and English silver is taken in trade with as much eagerness as is the Turkish piaster.

The British soldier, whatever changes may transpire elsewhere on the map of the Orient, has evidently chosen Egypt as a permanent place of abode.

The recent appointment of Mr. Ernest H. Crosby,

of New York, as Judge of the International Court at Alexandria, by President Harrison, was a judicious choice. The recognized Republican leader in the New York Assembly, his absence will be keenly felt—by his party comrades, especially. His scholarly tastes will find abundant scope for activity in his new field of labor, at all events.

Alexandria was founded by Alexander the Great, B. C. 332, from whom it derives its name. The re-opening of the Mahmoudieh Canal, in 1820, uniting the city with Rosetta, gave a fresh impetus to commerce, which has grown to enormous proportions since that period. The modern portion of the city covers the ancient island of Pharos, together with the isthmus connecting it with the main-land. It is a delightful winter resort, and the hotels are crowded during that season of the year.

Here, according to an attenuated tradition, the immense Alexandrian Library, consisting of seven hundred thousand valuable volumes, was burned by command of Caliph Omar, A. D. 643, on the ground that if they agreed with the Koran they were useless, while if they failed to harmonize with the book they deserved destruction. The story contains some improbable statements, and is doubted by many eminent scholars.

CHAPTER XIV.

DEPARTURE FROM EGYPT.—"BLUES" ON THE BLUE MEDITERRANEAN.—VIEWS OF STROMBOLI.—SARDINIA, CORSICA, MARSEILLES, LYONS, ETC.—THE CRETAN INSURRECTION.—ARRIVAL IN NEW YORK.—FAREWELL OBSERVATIONS.

ON the day of our departure from Alexandria for Marseilles the weather was cool and delightful. The broad streets and European aspect of this ancient city, after our wide and weary wanderings in many strange lands, proved exceptionally attractive and homelike. For the first time in our travels we were able to board the steamer without using the small boat manned by swaggering, swarthy, and swearing Turks or Arabs. Even at Liverpool we were compelled to take a lighter in order to disembark at the "landing stage" on our arrival from America.

Massive docks with derricks, tramways, and other appliances of modern civilization denoted alike the presence and plastic hand of England. A fleet of small boats surrounded our steamer as she lay securely moored at the pier, with a variety of Oriental wares and curios for sale. Some of them were sold at rates so ridiculously low as to excite the suspicion that they might be stolen goods—Turkish canes, convertible into pipes, for a franc—nineteen cents; the fez, or red cap, commonly worn in the East, for a similar sum, equal in quality to those purchased elsewhere on our journey for three times that amount. The most amazing bargain was a set of two necklaces and a pair of bracelets composed of minute shells—four distinct pieces—which were urged upon us at the nominal price of one English shilling, or twenty-four cents, for the entire lot!

Finally, our steamer got in motion, and the small army of peddlers disappeared. It was a French ship of the Messiariges Maritime Company, the same one, in fact, that conveyed our party from Jaffa to Port Said at the entrance of the famous Suez Canal. Since ships of this line spend from one to two days at each landing to receive or discharge freight, we had, meantime, visited all the points in Egypt covered by our itinerary at Port Said, Ismailia, Cairo, and Alexandria, and yet resumed our homeward passage on her.

Hitherto the Mediterranean had presented a placid and lamb-like appearance. Now she disclosed another and more repulsive phase of character. Before we were well out of the bay the sea became exceedingly choppy. The regular steamer had been taken off for the season and a much smaller one substituted, which rolled like an empty bottle. Much of the journey was of the same description. Soon many of our companions were in their berths, either positively sea-sick or too qualmish to notice objects of interest or discover any charm in the sonorous dinner-bell. The sea was blue, but they were "bluer" than the Mediterranean by far.

A portion of the deck cargo consisted of twenty-five hundred live quails caught in Egypt by nets. They were being taken to Paris to gratify the gastronomic instincts of that mercurial, polite, and pleasure-loving people. Much caution was necessary in moving about on the small steamer when she rolled to avoid being thrown on the top of a long line of fourth-class passengers sleeping on the deck in beds brought by them for the purpose. It is the poorest accommodation furnished, the passenger bringing his own food, though it is a very economical mode of traveling.

On the trip Crete is passed. The formidable insurrection against Turkish tyranny, which had been in progress for many months, was nearly subdued. The sympathy, if not practical aid, of Greece had done much to encourage the patriotic uprising and exasperate the Sublime Porte. Nothing less than a wholesome dread of the intervention of some one of the great European powers deterred the haughty Turk from punishing the Greeks for the attitude

OUR SHIP IN A GALE.

assumed by them. As it was, several sharp and significant threats were made toward Greece by the Turkish authorities to check the movement then in progress at Athens and elsewhere.

As a prudential measure the leaders of the insurrection, together with various other political offenders, were finally amnestied by the Sultan of Turkey, unless they had, previous to the outbreak, been tried and condemned. Of course, this will prove but a temporary suspension of hostilities. The cry for liberty is daily expanding. No temporary truce will avail either in Crete or elsewhere throughout the Turkish Empire. The potential hand on the dial of European statecraft points to the speedy overthrow of its cruel and blighting misrule.

Our route was through the Straits of Messina. On one side was the extreme southern point of Italy, and on the south the beautiful and balmy island of Sicily. The latter is famous for its oranges, lemons, almonds, olive-oil, maize, rice, barley, beans, pulse, manna, flax, licorice, and other productions. Her minerals include fine alabaster, sulphur, and several species of marble. The island is one hundred and eighty miles in length and one hundred miles wide at its broadest point. At the narrowest portion of the straits it is distant from Italy only two miles, to which country it politically belongs.

Its enormous fertility was duly recognized even in the days of Homer, who describes the inhabitants as follows:

> "Untaught to plant, to turn the glebe, and sow,
> They all their products to free nature owe;
> The soil untill'd, a ready harvest yields,
> With wheat and barley wave the golden fields;
> Spontaneous vines from weighty clusters pour,
> And Jove descends in each prolific shower."

According to Smyth the Sicilians "are of middle stature, well made, with dark eyes, and coarse black hair; their features are better than their complexions; and they attain maturity and begin to decline earlier than the inhabitants of more northern regions. They are cheerful, inquisitive, and fanciful, with a redundance of unmeaning compliments, showing that they are not so deficient in natural talents as in their proper cultivation. Their delivery is vehement, rapid, full of action, and their gesticulation violent; the latter is so significant as almost to possess the power of speech, and animates them with peculiar vivacity, bordering, however, rather on conceit than wit, on farce than humor.

"The upper classes are incorrigibly indolent and fond to excess of titles and such like marks of distinction. Here, in fact, every house is a palace, every handicraft is a profession, every respectable person at least an excellency, and every errand-boy is charged with an embassy! This love of ostentation is so inveterate that the poorer nobility and gentry are penurious in the extreme in their domestic arrangements, and almost starve themselves to be able to appear abroad in the evening in a poverty-stricken equipage."

MOONLIGHT ON THE MEDITERRANEAN.

Across the Tyrrhenian sea, amid much wild and stormy weather, with heavy waves, our little steamer sails on. Now the Strait of Bonifacio is reached, which separates the island of Sardinia from that of Corsica. The latter is distinguished as being the birthplace of Napoleon Bonaparte. He was born at

Ajaccio, the capital of that island, August 15, 1769. Here he remained until ten years of age, when he entered the military school at Brienne, an insignificant French town. The college was suppressed in 1790.

The French conquered Corsica in 1769, a few months before the birth of Bonaparte. Hence, had he been born previous to that event he would have been an Italian instead of a citizen of France. What effect, if any, nationality would have exerted over the man of destiny has long been a matter of speculation with many curious minds.

In religion Corsica is Roman Catholic, and in language Italian. It abounds in minerals, including lead, iron, antimony, granite, porphyry, jasper, and marble. Its forests are extensive, but agriculture is largely neglected. Wine is produced extensively, reaching often seven million gallons per annum. Fishing furnishes employment for many of the natives. Among the domestic animals used are the donkey, horse, mule, goat, and sheep. The climate is very mild, and during the winter months is the favorite resort of invalids. Steamers from Leghorn, Marseilles, and other ports make regular trips to the island.

Sardinia, situated on the southern side of the strait, is by far the most valuable island in the waters of the Mediterranean. Excelling in size all competitors, it produces annually large varieties of oranges, wine, wheat, barley, flax, hemp, tobacco, and other articles of commerce. Wild animals abound in the mountains especially.

Originally occupied by the ancient Phenicians and Etruscans, it has been held in succession by Greece, the Romans, Carthaginians, Spaniards, Germany, and now by Italy. During the summer months it is oppressively hot, making out-of-door life, when exposed to the rays of the sun, a source of positive discomfort, if not a menace to life itself. The winter is the most delightful season of the year. Its exports amount to about $2,500,000 annually, while its imports seldom exceed $2,000,000.

Two volcanoes are clearly visible from the deck of our steamer—Stromboli, on one of the Pilari Islands, between Sicily and the main coast of Italy, and Ætna, situated on the island of Sicily. Passing the former during the night, its bright fire of molten matter shone out to good advantage, though at so early an hour (about three o'clock in the morning) that it was witnessed by but comparatively few passengers. I beheld the spectacle with deep interest.

Ætna was passed during the day-time, hence the flames were nearly invisible. More than two thousand three hundred years ago its action was first noticed. Since that period successive generations of mankind have been swept away. Nations have arisen and crumbled back to dust. Still its lurid and awful light is constantly witnessed. Diodorus Siculus records its earliest activity, but fails, curiously enough, to furnish the date. According to Thucydides other extensive and startling eruptions occurred 475 and 425 B. C., respectively. Sixty distinct and disastrous ebullitions in all have been chronicled, the latest being in 1852, possibly the most terrific and destructive of all. The earthquake of 1669 was of a most alarming character. The entire village of Nicolosi was swept away, and from fissures in the mountain torrents of lava soon issued, which utterly destroyed fourteen thriving villages.

A disagreeable voyage of five days at length landed us in the beautiful and interesting city of Marseilles. Though our steamer came within two hundred feet of the pier, owing to the shallow water the inevitable small boat was again called into requisition to convey passengers to the shore. In the dense and dismal darkness of the night, amid a drizzling rain-storm, we slowly descended the slippery steps leading from the ship. At length all are ashore. Now comes the custom-house examination. All with souvenirs purchased in distant climes display some degree of nervous anxiety in view of the fact, and concerning the possible result of the rigid scrutiny.

The eloquence and blandishments of our accom-

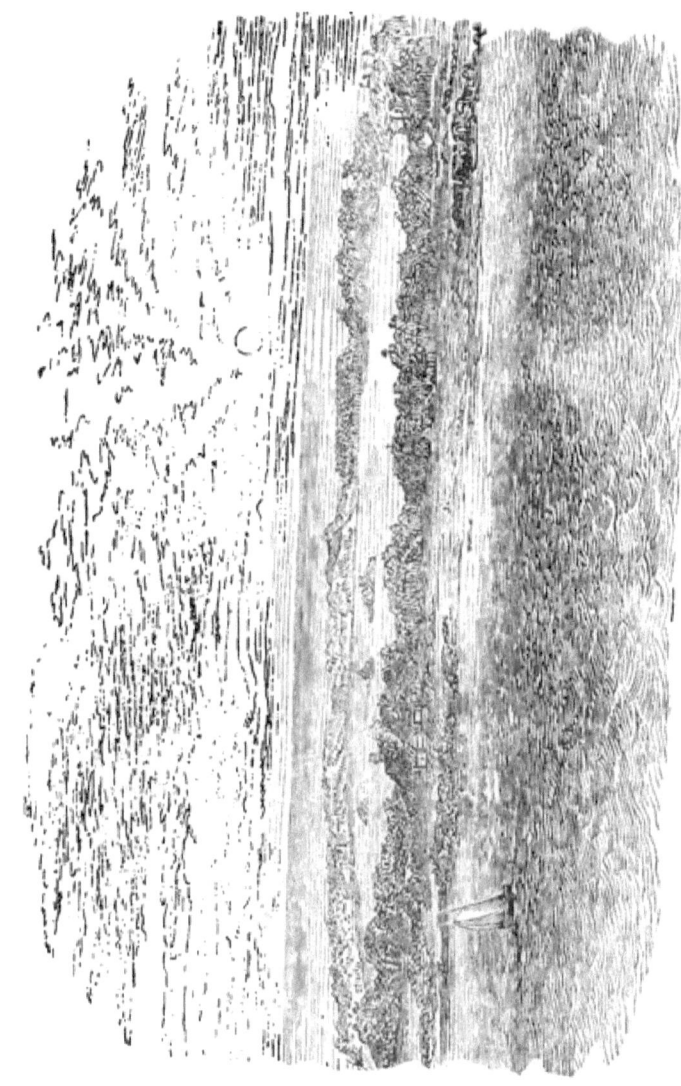

A CORAL ISLAND.

plished conductor, Professor R. H. Crunden, of London, achieve a marked victory. Probably a timely "tip" assists in the solution of the problem. At all events the luggage of the entire party is passed by the polite French officer in charge without a single piece being examined. "Beat that in America if you can," cried the professor, with a show of justifiable triumph. It would, indeed, be difficult to parallel the achievement in any country under the stars.

Since many of our party were anxious to catch the Guion steamer *Arizona* for New York, while others had short tours on the Continent or in Great Britain yet to make, we pushed perseveringly on to Paris, after a substantial supper and a short stroll about the city.

Marseilles presents numerous attractions to the average tourist, and is the chief sea-port of France. It is distant from Paris five hundred and thirty-four miles by railway, and includes the old as well as the beautiful and more modern town. The former has a labyrinth of narrow, filthy lanes and streets. Its trade in the Levant is very extensive, not to speak of its commercial relations with the United States and other lands. It is also the most important town in the Department of Bouches-du-Rhône. It was founded 600 B. C. by Aonian colonists from Asia Minor. A fine cathedral, besides other public buildings, fine boulevards, the beautiful and even the quaint architecture of the narrow streets, where *les miserables* endeavor to exist, possess varying degrees of interest. It was an all-night ride from Marseilles, with much needless discomfort in attempting to sleep, since the American sleeping-car is not generally adopted in Europe. Eastern nations, as a rule, forget nothing and learn new lessons slowly.

Lyons was reached in season for a late breakfast, and we are two hundred and twenty-two miles nearer Paris than when we left Marseilles the night before. The population of the city is placed at three hundred and fifty thousand. Many tall ungainly buildings are visible, a number of which are manufactories of some sort, the chief industry being the production of silk. Lyons is the leading manufacturing city in France. The amount of silk woven exceeds $40,000,000 annually. The industry was introduced into the place during the reign of Louis XI. by manufacturers from Lucca and Florence. An inferior quality of silk, though of strong texture, is produced expressly for sale in the United States.

It was after dark when our train reached Paris. An incessant ride of five hundred and thirty-four miles, with little sleep, and no opportunity for our customary ablutions, added to the trials of the journey. Lavatories on European or Asiatic trains are practically unknown. The traveler watches for an opportunity to leave the train at some principal station. Even then, unless warned by the leader of the party, he is in constant fear of being left behind. The station rooms are usually in charge of women, who guard and clean the premises, carefully exacting

LYONS.

about ten centimes (or two cents) from each customer.

One of our party, Mr. Andrew J. Hitt, of Kentucky, who had been ill since entering Palestine, was, at his own urgent request, left in Paris. We hoped to have taken him with us as far as London, if no farther, where he could converse in English. Every courtesy had been shown him by the guide of the party and all its members. A purse was made up to secure him a compartment on the train to Paris. Here he was left in the care of Dr. Warren, an eminent English-speaking physician, with all other needful provisions for his comfort. Here he rested for a few weeks, and finally returned to America with his health fully restored.

After a farewell stroll around the gay metropolis, including a parting view of the wonderful Eiffel Tower, with its wealth of brilliant and many-colored lights, we hastened on to London, where we arrived in the gray dawn of the following morning. The night passage across the English Channel was cheerless and the sea choppy. Since the miserable steamers are so small, the motion of the vessel was incessant, and many passengers were sea-sick. Why large and comfortable steamers are not placed on the route is a mystery to the American tourist.

Unfortunately, our closing day in London brought a cold drizzling rain. We suffered considerably from this change of weather, having so recently left Egypt with its mild temperature. Old points of interest, however, were revisited and new ones discovered and appreciated, various purchases made, and a midnight train taken for Liverpool. Three successive nights we had spent on railways without sleep, not including five days previously consumed in tossing on the wild waves of the wicked Mediterranean.

Nine days more conveyed us across the restless Atlantic and brought us to New York. Much of the passage was of a rough character. Opportunities for promenading on the deck were, in consequence, quite restricted. Reading, thorough resting after our interesting but wearisome travels, conversation, with impromptu concerts and recitations, utilized much of the spare time, not to mention three substantial meals daily. The humdrum of the monotonous life at sea was occasionally broken by sighting ships near at hand or remote on the very horizon. Schools of porpoises leaping from the water followed us eagerly ever and anon in pursuit of the garbage thrown overboard from the galleys.

A thrilling experience was reserved for us in mid-ocean. A steamer was on fire and signals of distress were displayed. Our ship hove to, and about two hours were spent in exchanging questions and answers offering assistance. The smoke could be distinctly seen pouring out in volumes fore and aft. It was the steamer *Queensmore*, a new vessel, and said to be on her first trip. Her cargo was composed largely of hay and horses. Finally, the captain of the unfortunate ship signaled that the fire was under control and assistance would not be needed.

VIEW OF THE OCEAN.

Then both steamers sailed away in opposite directions.

The captain of the *Queensmore*, however, was utterly mistaken; the fire was not extinguished. After smoldering a few hours it broke out again. It was fought furiously for several days. At length the ill-fated vessel was run ashore on the Irish coast, where she burned to the water's edge. All the officers and crew happily succeeded in making their escape. The closing particulars we learned from the public press a few days after reaching home.

Of course, all custom-house examinations are more or less exasperating. They try one's nerve, pocket-book, and religion. Nowhere is so rigid a scrutiny made as in the United States, not excepting Turkey itself. America requires the traveler to make his declaration in writing and under oath. Then to show that he is not believed, even under oath, his baggage is overhauled in the search for smuggled goods. Scholars, statesmen, clergymen, coal-heavers, and hod-carriers are subjected to the same needless and shameful indignity. Surely, some modification of the law is most imperatively and promptly demanded.

Aside from this criticism, however, it is a mere truism to declare, as I do, that America possesses unrivaled and wonderful natural, social and commercial, ecclesiastical and political advantages, superior by far to any country existing on the face of the globe. Like ancient Jerusalem, it is "the joy of the whole earth." To proclaim yourself an American while traveling, even in the most remote and semi-barbarous regions of the earth, elicits greater respect and awe than the talismanic cry in the palmy days of the Roman Empire: "I am a Roman citizen." Every-where the term "American" is regarded as symbolical of liberty, with a free press, free thought, and boundless possibilities for domestic and national advancement. By the masses he is deemed either a millionaire or a fool. No other conclusion can they arrive at, in view of his prodigal use of money in traveling to distant lands, and freely giving it away for views of old ruins and in the purchase of articles of curiosity.

To fully appreciate the inestimable and unique advantages of our own land, therefore, it is not enough to merely visit prominent points of interest with which the United States abound, as some with great simplicity suggest. That is important. But one must witness the squalor and degradation of the Old World, its low wages, caste, and a thousand and one hoary, hateful, and absurd customs, its fading grandeur and regal splendors, turbulent and hungry masses, with tottering thrones, to recognize fully the true dignity and value of American manhood.

After four visits to Canada and two to Europe, seeing all phases of life in England, Scotland, Ireland, France, Belgium, Germany, Holland, Switzerland, Italy, Greece, Turkey, Palestine, and Egypt, we comprehend in a loftier degree than ever before the amazing and pre-eminent advantages of the United States of America. With the familiar lines of Longfellow, therefore, we may appropriately close and bid the patient and thoughtful reader a long farewell.

> "Thou, too, sail on, O ship of state!
> Sail on, O Union, strong and great!
> Humanity with all its fears,
> With all the hopes of future years
> Is hanging breathless on thy fate!
> We know what master laid thy keel,
> What workman wrought thy ribs of steel,
> Who made each mast and sail and rope,
> What anvils rang, what hammers beat,
> In what a forge and what a heat,
> Were shaped the anchors of thy hope!
> Fear not each sudden sound and shock,
> 'Tis of the wave and not the rock,
> 'Tis but the flapping of the sail,
> And not a rent made by the gale!
> In spite of rock and tempest's roar,
> In spite of false lights on the shore,
> Sail on, nor fear to breast the sea!
> Our hearts, our hopes, are all with thee,
> Our hearts, our hopes, our prayers, our tears,
> Our faith triumphant o'er our fears,
> Are all with thee—are all with thee."

www.ingramcontent.com/pod-product-compliance
Lightning Source LLC
Chambersburg PA
CBHW030810230426
43667CB00008B/1146